Class and Gender in
Early English Literature

Class and Gender in Early English Literature

INTERSECTIONS

* * * * *

EDITED BY

Britton J. Harwood

AND

Gillian R. Overing

INDIANA UNIVERSITY PRESS
Bloomington and Indianapolis

The paper used in this publication meets the minimum requirements of
American National Standard for Information Sciences—Permanence
of Paper for Printed Library Materials, ANSI Z39.48-1984.
⊗ ™

Manufactured in the United States of America

Library of Congress Cataloging-in-Publication Data

Class and gender in Early English literature : intersections / edited
by Britton J. Harwood and Gillian R. Overing.
    p.   cm.
    Includes index.
    ISBN 0-253-32734-2. — ISBN 0-253-20858-0 (pbk.)
    1. English literature—Middle English, 1100–1500—History and
criticism.   2. English literature—Old English, ca. 450–1100—
History and criticism.   3. Literature and society—England—History.
4. Social classes in literature.   5. Sex role in literature.
I. Harwood, Britton J. II. Overing, Gillian R., date.
PR275.S63C57   1994
820.9′355—dc20   93-14471
            1 2 3 4 5 99 98 97 96 95 94

Contents

Foreword

✳ ✳ ✳

Britton J. Harwood
Gillian R. Overing

This volume is part of an ongoing conversation—among a group of medievalists and a variety of perspectives. Some of the writers in this collection have worked and talked together before, and others came together at the 26th International Medieval Congress at Western Michigan University with the express purpose of developing a working exchange as a group. When we requested three consecutive sessions at the Congress, we had in mind a kind of mini-seminar, a process of exchange and a development of viewpoints—a series of intersections. We had asked participants to be prepared to address issues of class if they had focused on gender, and vice versa, and to think in terms of the intersections of these two issues throughout the three sessions, taking the view that texts/subjects that might seem to offer themselves more readily to one form of analysis might be even more valuably examined from the other. "Feminist criticism, for example, is especially important for works which ignore feminist issues," Jonathan Culler suggests, as "the value of the theoretical orientation is its bringing to light of what is unsaid or unthought in a particular work."[1] We had been concerned to cross and even break down "territorial" boundaries—some participants who had worked primarily in Old English had taken on Middle English texts, and vice versa—and we were inviting a self-conscious examination of each participant's own critical practice. The volume reflects the questions and issues that the writers brought to the exchange, and those that developed as a result of it.

Each chapter, written especially for the anthology, contains its individual author's conscious examination of the shared problematic of the collection as a whole. Consequently, in our introduction, we have chosen to discuss in a more general way some aspects of this shared problematic and of our progress as a group of scholars with similar concerns. We thought this approach more useful and appropriate than the more traditional editorial "listing" of the particular contribution of each essay.

The impetus for requesting these special sessions came from our agreement that the analysis of literary texts as a place of class but not gender conflict, like the analysis of gender relations to the neglect of class, is problematic. However convenient genderless classes might be to Marxist analysis, "Fiction refuses the notion of genderless class subjectivity," as Cora Kaplan has pointed out.[2] Essentializing the feminine (or masculine), however, without regard for the historical location or situation of actual men and women, would simply resituate some persistent exclusions and familiar questions.

We began by trying to isolate what was problematic and to articulate it as *the* problematic for the group. In doing so we discovered that while gender and class have become important critical issues for medievalists, the intersection of these two issues has received only sporadic attention overall, and very little attention within the medieval period. There is a developing body of critical work on medieval women, and a number of essay collections focusing on women in Old and Middle English literature, although it remains true that the early medieval period has received less critical attention overall. Most recently Helen Damico and Alexandra Hennessey Olsen's *New Readings on Women in Old English Literature* (Indiana University Press, 1990) brings together a variety of essays, most of them previously published, which primarily serve to chronicle the historical development of critical attention and inattention to gender in this period. Such collections as *New Images of Medieval Women* (ed. Edelgard E. DeBruck, Mellen, 1989) or *Ambiguous Realities: Women in the Middle Ages and Renaissance* (ed. Carole Levin and Jeanie Watson, Wayne State University Press, 1987) remain focused on literary contexts of female representation and are less concerned with socially constructed aspects of gender.

There are of course literary scholars engaged in social and theoretical analysis of medieval literature (for example, Sheila Delany, *Medieval Literary Politics*, Manchester University Press, 1990), and there are essay collections which reflect this engagement. *Medieval Literature: Criticism, Ideology and History* (ed. David Aers, St. Martin's Press, 1986) and *Speaking Two Languages: Traditional Disciplines and Contemporary Theory in Medieval Studies* (ed. Allen Frantzen, SUNY Press, 1991) are two such anthologies concerned with addressing issues of both class and gender. But in order to find even partial attempts at a specific and conscious connection between the issues of gender and class one must look, apparently, to medieval historians.

Recent essay collections in medieval history reflect a new emphasis on the cultural and political contexts of gender and class issues. Some noteworthy examples include *Women in Medieval History and Historiography* (ed. Susan Mosher Stuard, University of Pennsylvania Press, 1987), *Women and Power in the Middle Ages* (ed. Mary Erler and Maryanne Kowaleski, University of Georgia Press, 1988) and *Sisters and Workers in the Middle Ages* (ed. Judith M. Bennett et al., University of Chicago Press, 1989). Some anthologies combine literary and historical analyses—for example, *Women in the Middle Ages and the Renaissance: Literary and Historical Perspectives* (ed. Mary Beth Rose, Syracuse University Press, 1986) and *Widowhood* (ed. Louise Mirrer, University of Michigan Press, 1992). These studies, while valuable, are either primarily gender-focused or tend to deal separately with literary and historical constructs of gender and class.

As we set out to outline and define the problematic for our conference group in a relative critical vacuum, our attempts at definition became instead a series of questions: Is psychoanalysis the most promising site of intersection, with its insistence that sexual identity develops inseparably from an always historically specific or social placement? If concern for a link between class and gender must be materialist from the beginning, does patriarchy have its own material base? As a system, does it always have reciprocal relations with a structure of social classes? Or, to the contrary, is feudal patriarchy a single system, with the consequence that, in order to understand male dominance of women as essential to the entire system (not just the family), analysis must be reconceived, perhaps with (gender) division of labor introduced as a category no less fundamental than class?

We also asked, "Does the medieval period pose in a *distinctive* way the question of a link between class and gender?" For example, the politics of the European middle ages are distinguished at least partly by the facts, first, that the political is not constructed within feudalism as distinct from the economic and, second, that the economic (as the site of the production of food and other objects) is chiefly the family. But the medieval family is also the site of biological (re)production, of course. Hence, to a significant degree, the "political 'instance' " in the medieval period does not exist outside the same sphere in which gender emerges.

The distinctiveness of this by contrast with the modern period is immediately apparent. Where, within capitalism, the political is constructed as a public space in which the gender of citizens is eventually stipulated as irrelevant, sexuality and desire are assigned to a private sphere, constructed within capitalist ideology as driving the market. Consequently, within capitalism, class, so far as it has a political valence, is constructed in opposition to gender; and the scholarly work of linkage, therefore, must be a deconstructive labor.

The tangle with which material production and biological (re)production present themselves in the middle ages invites a much different inquiry. To begin with, peasant men and women had (as Barbara Hanawalt remarks) "few economic options outside of establishing a family unit." Agricultural labor, the basis of ninety percent of late-medieval European wealth, was divided along gender lines. In Hanawalt's summary, "the husbandman's work was chiefly in field and forest while women worked mostly about the home."[3] Meanwhile, family members are not always easy to distinguish from unrelated employees: the "servant" recorded as living in the house of a manorial tenant may be either the tenant's son or the son of another tenant or an unrelated and landless wage-laborer. Because customary tenants are in effective possession of much of the land, they make up an appreciable political force, separable only in analysis from the peasant's economic position. This position materially coincides with the sphere of biological (re)production. Hence, the political position of peasants is only analytically separable from their gendered position within (re)production.

Gender and class coincide no less within medieval aristocracies. The kinship system that enforced the transfer of a woman from one man to another man traced out a path for the movement of wealth—preeminently land. Where, within capitalism, consumption is largely gendered as female, the well-born woman within feudalism is assimilated to the surplus product, the object to be (conspicuously) consumed. Her (re)productive labor becomes a means of maintaining a claim on the surplus of the productive labor of tenants.

If we attribute to Old and Middle English literature not just a material history of their own but a function in the material history where class and gender emerge, then the specific interaction of class and gender in precapitalist Europe calls for literary study that takes it into account. A brief example may make this clear.

A case can be made that the reversal of gender roles—the empowerment of the women—distinguishing the poetry of *fin amor*, 'courtly love', arises, as certain ritual structures do, within a culture torn by rival authorities and decentralized polity. The *domina* of courtly love appears to be a double negation: as empowered, she negates the woman who is the object rather than the agent of an economic transfer. As desirable, however, she also negates the woman who is merely a term within the Law (the woman as what must be transferred). She witnesses to the Law she negates, since desire is the outcome of the Law. Thus, study of *fin amor* as representation must evidently take into account the particular coincidence of the fused economic and political power operated by noble males. This fusion is precisely a system of kinship, within which gender is constructed. Moreover, such study must take this fusion into account precisely by describing how this coincidence comes to be represented by a specific poetry of sexual desire.

Nor does this poetry fail to intervene within feudalism in a wider sense. The very high incidence of marriage among peasants testifies to economic expediency: only the tenant (not the cottar or other landless laborers) can hope for a retainable surplus; and tenancies imply the need for a family. That gender roles are defined outside of marriage in the poetry of *fin amor* therefore inscribes the necessity of marriage within the field of the other. *Libeaus desconus,* the 'beautiful unknown', is only apparently servile, the servile appearing in the poetry of *fin amor* only as brutal, if it appears at all.

That such poetry may function within the rest of material history does not mean that it succeeds in silencing the contradictions of feudalism, where an exploiting class, with its own coincidence of the gendered and economic, has one measure of political power, and an exploited class, with a different such coincidence, exerts political power of its own. These contradictions may be represented by, if not reflected in, the reversal of gender roles in courtly love. In fact, the poetry of *fin amor* may function in part to contain them. These contradictions would seem to call for an attentiveness to the interrelations between class and gender throughout the whole social formation, even as this poetry points to such an interrelationship within the exploiting class itself.

The distinctive dimensions of interrelationships like this one, both within the medieval period and for medievalists themselves, became further apparent at the 1991 Congress. When this diverse group of scholars came together, the questions multiplied and the problematic became more so. Our task changed and diversified as we progressed. In fact, anxiety about any attempt at intersecting gender and class analysis *became* to some extent the problematic itself. We hear the terms "gender" and "class" paired often, and the juxtaposition, as a member of our audience at one of the sessions pointed out, can resound as a part of an unexamined critical litany. We were obliged in practice to examine the practice of intersection itself. Even deciding on the order of these chapters raised mundane and practical questions about how we perceived intersection. We eventually decided to order the chapters with several different principles in mind; we sought a balance and an alternation between male and female authors, between Old and Middle English periods, and between those chapters that were primarily concerned with elucidating points of rhetoric and sign systems, and those that were more concerned with the function of the text within material history. When we pair these issues, do we necessarily conflate them and thereby dull or remove a specific edge in the interests of some homogeneous marginality? A marginality that might leave social constructs of masculinity unexamined, not to mention the varieties of social classes? Or do we pair them in confrontational fashion? How, then, to rank, how to decide on the value of competing schools of theory? "Can one set of terms be mapped onto another, and if so, how?" asks Culler. "Is one set reducible to another? Which is more 'basic'?"[4] Culler calls attention to the problems inherent in the very language of these last questions and asserts the difficulties of maintaining clear priorities in one's "choice" of theory: "We are ineluctably both in language and history. Nor, it appears, can we escape being gendered subjects or placed in some race, however defined. These are not alternatives among which one can choose. . . ."[5] Indeed, if one issue becomes set against the other when marginality and forms of oppression are the central preoccupations of each, does the question then become what does the analyst of class *have to lose* to the analyst of gender, or vice versa, and to what extent do the realities of our own lives as medieval scholars condition this oppositionality? The point of intersection is the point of most discomfiture because it is also the point of least resolution. And to investigate the site of this discomfort is also to investigate the speaker.

Critical texts are cultural products like texts of other kinds, of course. If they somehow escape ideology, how do they manage this? If they do not, and if we as scholars are no less implicated in class and gender relations than the persons and texts that we write about, is there any interesting way in which our criticism can disclose its own function within social contestation? Our own class and gender identities and those in the medieval fictions that we study are bound in a web of oppositions and interconnections that confrontational or exclusionary logic will not illuminate. The practice of intersection can be, and indeed should be, distinguished from the practice of opposition. To intersect suggests a passage, an active passing through and between, establishing multiple points of contact and divergence. With this model in mind, this collection seeks to articulate some sites of intersection, to provide a meeting ground, a place of convergence—one which aims to illuminate the intersections of methodology, critic, and medieval text.

Notes

1. "Literary Theory," in *Introduction to Scholarship in Modern Languages and Literatures,* ed. Joseph Gibaldi (New York: Modern Language Association, 1992), 225.

2. *Sea Changes: Essays on Culture and Feminism* (London: Verso, 1986), 165.

3. *The Ties That Bound: Peasant Families in Medieval England* (New York: Oxford University Press, 1986), 113. The estimate of the basis of European wealth is M. M. Postan's, in "Economic Foundations of Medieval Society," in his *Essays on Medieval Agriculture and General Problems of the Medieval Economy* (Cambridge, England: Cambridge University Press, 1973), 22.

4. "Literary Theory," 216.

5. "Literary Theory," 217.

Class and Gender in
Early English Literature

Gender, Sexual Violence, and the Politics of War in the Old English *Judith*

* * *

Karma Lochrie

With cultural legislation comes cultural legibility, or illegibility—and then comes, inevitably, the collective and individual paranoia on which much social and psychic life depends.[1]

Gender and class are but two categories of identity and social organization which structure our thinking and living, as well as our reading of medieval texts. Along with race, ethnicity, and sexuality, these categories interdependently organize social hierarchies, individual identities, and cultural relations of power. The interdependence of these categories is not only the principle that reinforces their power and invisibility, but it is also, paradoxically, what makes them vulnerable. When the borderlines of these definitional categories become ambiguous, Marjorie Garber has argued, we can observe the crisis of these same categories.[2] Gender and class, as interdependent categories, both reinforce and worry each other because they rely on each other for security. A crisis in one precipitates a crisis "elsewhere."

Any intersection of categories invokes just such a crisis. An interrogation of the intersection of class and gender in medieval texts is therefore not likely to produce either a harmonious or a resolved reading. As a principle of investigating these categories, intersection implies all the violence and disturbance that is bound to occur when the boundaries which define cultural categories are crossed. By intersecting the categories of gender and class, we are not only seeking a kind of legibility of medieval culture: we are also striving to make visible the

regulatory effects of these categories on individual and collective identities. At stake in our readings are our own boundaries of legibility—of
medieval texts and cultures—and our own susceptibility to that "collective and individual paranoia" which accompanies the discovery of
illegibility of those very categories on which we depend as individuals
and from which we make our livelihood as scholars.

I would like to adapt the terms of our intersected readings to my
study of the Anglo-Saxon poem *Judith* by revising the category of class
to its military and social cousin, the category of rank.[3] This revision of
terms is necessitated by the world of the poem, a military order under
the leadership of Holofernes/Judith which is explicitly structured according to rank, rather than class. Gender enters this order initially in
its proper "place," that is, as a subset of the military system of rank
asserted in Holofernes's camp. However, in the course of the poem, the
two categories become increasingly confused, and gender comes to displace rank in the literal intersection ("cutting off" or "between") of
Holofernes's head.

The occasion for the confusion of categories is a dual one of the upcoming battle between the Assyrians and Bethulians and of rape. As a
ritual assertion of masculine-bonding in his military community and as
a premature enjoyment of the spoils of victory over the Bethulians, the
Assyrian commander, Holofernes, plans to rape Judith. It is the despoil-
ing and inversion of that rape which precipitates the crisis of categories—of gender and military rank—and which exposes the alliance
between the economies of war and sexual violence in the world of the
poem and, by implication, Anglo-Saxon society.

The Old English *Judith* has always resisted the efforts of Anglo-
Saxonists applying traditional methods of inquiry that would reduce
it to the univocity of their methods. Source studies comparing the
poem to the *Liber Iudith* of the Vulgate, allegorical and tropological
interpretations, thematic studies derived from heroic typologies, and
textual analysis have produced a variety of readings of this poem as
"a typological portrait of heroic virtue," a celebration of female chastity, and a dramatic rendering of the victory of the Church over the
Devil.[4]

David Chamberlain and Alexandra Hennessey Olsen have used some
of the same methods to argue that "those who allegorize *Judith* may be
misinterpreting the poem" because they ignore the clear political purpose behind it: to inspire the English to rise up against the Danes. According to their analyses, the intended rape of Judith serves to remind

the English audience of the Danish invaders' widespread rape of Anglo-Saxon women described by Wulfstan. Her heroic spoiling of Holofernes's plans offers a model for political action. Ælfric refers to just such a political motive behind one version of the _Judith_, which was intended "as an example to men to defend our land against the assailing army."[5] The historical and political urgency of the Judith story, according to this analysis, would not have been lost on the Anglo-Saxons, even if it is subsumed and effectively erased under modern attempts of scholars to allegorize the poem.

The conflicting claims of allegorical and political readings of the _Judith_ poem question the whole project of this volume, that is, the "intersectability" of diverse modes of reading. Those who argue for an allegorical reading of the poem often ignore the political and historical implications, while those who insist on a political reading maintain that such a reading is incompatible with allegory.[6] At the heart of this disagreement is a question about methods of reading. Allegorical readers of the poem usually fail to examine the cultural assumptions they bring to their analysis, particularly the self-perpetuating nature of the allegorical paradigm. Based as allegorical reading is on the identification of sources and relevant commentary (often biblical), it relies on the reconstructed background of a text for its commentary—textual and literary—of that text.[7] Not only does this practice render political and social contexts irrelevant to the act of interpretation; it privileges sources over the texts being studied. This leads, in the case of the _Judith_ poem, to the reading of its biblical source _into_ the Old English poem. Thus, where the two texts diverge in their representations of Judith, biblical commentaries are called in to provide the material which is lacking. For example, the biblical text stresses Judith's chaste widowhood, while the Old English poem does not. The biblical source and the commentaries of Jerome and Isidore of Seville and Aldhelm's _De Virginitate_ are brought to bear on the poem to restore the tropological reading of Judith as a figure of chastity where it is lacking in the Anglo-Saxon. Source study is not, of course, an approach which is unique to the Old English _Judith;_ it is a common methodology for reading Anglo-Saxon prose as well as poetry—so common, in fact, that it has become an authorizing system in Anglo-Saxon scholarship.[8]

Scholars do not stop at interpreting _Judith_ in terms of its sources. They perform textual reconstructions on it so that the poem more closely coheres with its biblical "original." The fact that _Judith_ is a fragment—that it lacks a beginning—seems to invite such reconstruc-

tion, at least among those who view Anglo-Saxon texts as pale reflections of their origins. The reasoning behind such reconstruction is as
self-perpetuating as it is unself-reflecting: *good* Anglo-Saxon poems
accurately reflect their original source(s). A poem which does not is not
good, and is in need of revision. The textual "lack" provides the obvious occasion—indeed, invitation—to the scholar to supply the original that is wanting to make the poem a good poem. This, in turn, leads
to speculation about the missing beginning that would have compen-
sated for that "certain sense of structural misproportion" in the Old
English poem due to its incongruity with the biblical version. Finally,
the poem is reconciled to its source, but only after 850–950 lines have
been hypothesized for it, making it more aesthetic, more dramatic, and
more meaningful than the surviving Anglo-Saxon poem, according to
one scholar's judgment.[9]

Such approaches to the poem and to other Old English texts like it
often do ignore political analysis. At the same time, though, the political reading of this poem is equally prohibitive in its assumption of re-
alism as the motivation behind the politics. The poem is made to depict
a "realistic situation," which accurately reflects historical circumstances. Thus, Holofernes's intended rape of Judith comes to stand for
actual rapes occurring in England during the late tenth and early eleventh century—actual, that is, if we are to believe Wulfstan.

Neither view of the poem, as a reflection of "reality" or as a sum of
its sources, allows for any investigation of the cultural or ideological
positioning of the text of the Old English *Judith*. Both methods are
"preemptive," to borrow the language of Lee Patterson in describing
some historical methods, that is, they prohibit anything but a reflec-
tionist view of the text in relation either to "reality" or to its
"sources."[10] Furthermore, both are preemptive in their totalizing visions of textual meaning and in their unself-reflecting critical positions.
The exegetical and historical material brought to bear on the poem
is presented with a self-evidence that leaves no room for personal re-
actions to the poem. Thus, Burton Raffel's "sense of disquiet—sometimes reaching rather intense levels" about "something . . . not quite
right" in the Old English *Judith*—a perception recently echoed by
John P. Hermann—is subsumed under the various extratextual strategies for producing meaning in the poem.[11]

I would like to begin with this "something" that is not quite right in
the poem, and venture to suggest that something is not quite right be-

cause of an intersection of categories in the poem—of gender and social rank—which produces a crisis. In all the discussions of Judith's decapitation of Holofernes, never has the action been examined in terms of these twin categories of gender and social rank, much less of either alone. Although most scholars consider the threatened rape of Judith and decapitation of Holofernes as central to the poem, no one has considered what the gendered implications of these twin actions are beyond the representation of Judith as a strong woman.[12] Sexual violence occupies a key position in the poem, yet scholars seem unwilling to investigate the ideology employed in its representation. Likewise, the relationship between this sexual violence and the politics of war as it is played out between the Assyrians and the Bethulians is rarely considered. I would like to suggest that the poem is unsettling because of the way in which it juxtaposes sexual violence with the politics of war. Further, I think it has troubling things to say about the intersection of the cultural categories of gender and military hierarchy in Anglo-Saxon culture, whether the poem specifically addresses the conflict with the Danish invaders or not. And finally, I want to offer some disturbing intersections between the cultural politics of gender and war in the Anglo-Saxon poem and in our contemporary society.

The conjunction of gender and the politics of war may be seen in the opening scene of Holofernes's feast. The traditional, ritualistic function of the pre-battle feast is, according to Gillian Overing, the establishment of a masculine speech community through various kinds of speech acts, such as boasts, oaths of loyalty, and declarations of gratitude, greeting, and praise.[13] It is through such speech acts that the warrior community prepares itself for battle by invoking deeds of bravery, heroic genealogies, and the social values of fame and honor which justify such deeds. Yet, the line between these speech acts and the violence they celebrate is often crossed, causing the rupture of the very community they are intended to reinforce. The outburst of Unferth at Hrothgar's feast before Grendel's attack is just one example of how speech acts intended to solidify the community topple over into violence.

Holofernes's feast treads this line more dangerously. While he encourages his men to "bear themselves well" in the upcoming battle, he abdicates his role as speaker in this community by engaging in riotous excess. The text of the poem emphasizes not the voices of warriors pro-

claiming their loyalties, but the inarticulate and violent sounds of
Holofernes's drunkenness:

> Ða wearð Holofernus,
> goldwine gumena,   on gytesalum,
> hloh ond hlydde,   hlynede ond dynede,
> þæt mihten fira bearn   feorran gehyran
> hu se stiðmoda   styrmde ond gylede,
> modig ond medugal,   manode geneahhe
> bencsittende   þæt hi gebærdon wel.
> (Then was Holofernes,
> the gold-friend of men,   into his cups,
> he laughed and clamored,   roared and shouted,
> so that the sons of men could   hear for miles
> how the stern one   stormed and yelled,
> proud and drunk,   frequently exhorted
> his feasting companions   that they conduct themselves well.)[14]

Instead of speech acts by means of which the male community prepares
itself for war, Holofernes's feast is characterized by the far-reaching
sounds of laughing, clamoring, and storming. There is a masculine
bonding apparent in Holofernes's exhortation to his comrades amidst
the drunkenness and festivity; however, it is marked not by the cere-
monial idioms of the war community but by the collapse of language in
a performance of masculine riot. Holofernes is the image, according to
Hermann, of "hypertrophied masculinity," a parody of the masculine
ideals of governance, loyalty, fealty, and power, as well as the language
that insures these ideals.[15]
    It is a mistake, though, to view the Old English representation of
Holofernes simply as a figuration of pride, arrogance, and worldliness,
as it is usually viewed in allegorical interpretations of the poem. There
is, to borrow Raffel's word, "something" about this feast that is as
comfortable in the world of the warrior community as it is in allegorical representations of vainglory. Hrothgar's feasts share in some of the
revelry we find among Holofernes's bench-sitters. In Heorot before
Grendel's attack, the evening's festivities are marked by the sounds of
warriors laughing and loud voices, just as later, before Wealhtheow's
speech, the "bench-noise" characterizes Heorot's social community.[16]
Even a clearly allegorical poem like the Old English *Vainglory* associ-
ates the warrior community with these sounds of joy (in Hrothgar's
hall) and riotous excess (in Holofernes's), whereby the speeches be-

come indistinguishable from the clamor of hypertrophied masculinity.[17] The dangers of vainglory, pride, and excess are linked in these texts with the celebrations of masculinity and war occasioned by the Anglo-Saxon feast.

Whatever they may allegorically represent, the codes of Holofernes's feast—its speeches, boasts, even its excesses—are the legible, legitimizing signs of warrior status in Anglo-Saxon culture. Hypertrophied though this representation is, it is not too far removed from those feasts which serve their ritualistic purpose of preparing for war by solidifying the male community. At the same time, the poem begins to encode a warning against this same social system. The effect of its rhetorical hypertrophy is to underscore the dangers of these masculine rituals, in particular, the threats of violence and the breakdown of language. The depiction of Holofernes's feast is thus haunted by the more temperate and orderly feasts of Anglo-Saxon literature and culture, pointing to the more disturbing aspects of this masculine ritual which will culminate in Holofernes's plan to rape Judith. A crisis is precipitated by the *excess* of the feast, even though this excess is endemic to the feast and the social system it celebrates. Excess is thus the principle which proves the undoing—the crisis—of Holofernes's world, for it produces a slippage of gender and rank—two categories he has endeavored to manipulate in his role as military commander.

Holofernes's feast is also marked by the absence of women, as compared with the biblical story of *Judith*, in which the heroine is actually present. Indeed, most Anglo-Saxon feasts feature women in the ritualistic role of passing the cup, praising the deeds of men, and reminding the community of its filial obligations, as Wealhtheow does in *Beowulf*. The absence of women from Holofernes's feast not only contributes to the representation of hypertrophied masculinity in the poem, but it comments on the homosocial structure of the Assyrian military community. I use this term, homosocial, as Eve Kosofsky Sedgwick has defined it, to refer to "social bonds between persons of the same sex," which we call male-bonding today.[18] Even where women are present, as Overing has very cogently argued, their participation in the speech community is different than that of the men.[19] While the loud clamor and drunkenness of Holofernes's feast are clearly not the representative or exemplary speech-acts of the socially constitutive Anglo-Saxon feast, they exist nevertheless on the continuum of masculine bonding. The noises of revelry exemplify more than Holofernes's pride: they are the audible effects of the violence subsumed and controlled by the rituals of the festive speech community. The violence underlying and informing the ritual of social interaction in a masculine economy erupts in the feast, causing a breakdown of language into a masculine hysterics marked by clamor, storming, laughter, and raucous speech.

The social implications of Holofernes's feast that I have been describing, that is, the exposure of the homosocial community and the discourse of violence that engenders it, are not to be found in the biblical version of the story. In the Book of Judith, the feast is described merely as a "supper for the servants" where Holofernes "was made merry" and "drank exceeding much wine" (12:10, 20). The role of the feast in the masculine warrior economy is the subject of the Old English poem, not its biblical source. The *Judith* poet thus repositions the story, particularly Holofernes's actions, within a new context which implicates Anglo-Saxon culture over and above the personal sins of Holofernes. Carnal desire proves to be a function not only of Holofernes's pride and drunkenness, but of a masculine warrior economy bound by a homosocial network and a code of violence that does not always succeed in masking the sexual aggression it sublimates.

"And the heart of Holofernes was smitten, for he was burning with the desire of her" (Judith 12:16). The Old English *Judith* alters the desire of Holofernes from one which began with a smitten heart to a desire positioned between the ritual of social bonding and preparations for war. Unlike the biblical Holofernes, the Anglo-Saxon leader desires to defile Judith in the "natural" progression of things which leads from revelry with his male retinue to rape and, finally, to war:

> Þa wearð se brema on mode
> bliðe, burga ealdor,   þohte ða beorhtan idese
> mid widle ond mid womme besmitan. . . . (57b–59)
>> (Then was the famous lord of cities
> happy in mind,   he planned to defile
> the shining woman with filth and stains. . . .)

The fantasy of a proud man drunk with wine, this is also the desire produced by the economy of masculine revelry and rivalry celebrated in the feast and reinforced through heroic deeds in war.

Rank enters the poem as a category which gives Holofernes's world meaning and which collides with the categories of gender and sexuality at the site of Holofernes's bed. It is here that Holofernes conducts his military campaign, and here, too, that the violence of masculine subjectivity is vividly emblematized. His bed is surrounded by a beautiful golden net so that, the text tells us, he could look upon anyone entering his room without their being able to see him unless he decided to speak with them (46–54). Holofernes exercises his power by means of the masculine gaze. In _Speculum of the Other Woman_, Luce Irigaray reveals how the gaze functions to define the masculine subject by objectifying others and arrogating to itself the prerogative of looking. Subjectivity, authority, and power are constituted through the gaze, while the feminine is objectified and made a spectacle—or mirror—of masculinity.[20] As a means of asserting mastery and authority, the gaze "enacts the voyeur's desire for sadistic power, in which the object of the gaze is cast as its passive, masochistic, feminine victim," in the words of Toril Moi.[21] Holofernes is, in fact, a self-styled voyeur who commands through the veil of his voyeurism. Gazing on his subordinates, he plays the part of voyeur by forcing them into the role of the feminine, passive victim of the masculine gaze. His activity thus encodes military rank in gendered and sexualized terms. Whether he is exerting mastery over his retinue, seeking to subdue the Bethulians, or planning to rape Judith, it is by means of this voyeuristic gaze. In this brief description of Holofernes's bed with its veiled canopy, the Old English text exposes the nexus of power relationships—military and sexual—that makes legible the masculine heroic economy.

Even more significantly in view of the heroic code associated with war in Anglo-Saxon culture, this portrait of the gaze positions Holofernes's desire for Judith within a larger masculine scheme of violence. The Old English Holofernes is smitten by a masculine subjectivity predicated on the violence of the gaze, not by the radiant beauty of Judith. The poem, in effect, recasts his desires against the violence of the warrior economy in which he thrives.

Understood in the context of this practice of ruling and violating by means of the gaze, the decapitation of Holofernes signifies its reversal and spoiling. Instead of defiling Judith as he had planned, Holofernes falls senseless to the bed, overcome with wine. Presumably, he never even sees Judith. Instead, she sees him. Holofernes becomes the object of her gaze, and this is the subtext of this decapitation. Judith is able to refuse the gaze, to turn it back on itself, and to appropriate its violence. In this respect, she bears more of a comparison with the violent Modthryth in _Beowulf_, who also refuses the masculine gaze by punishing any man who looks at her with death, than she does with any of the holy women or heroic men with whom she is usually compared.[22]

Judith's appropriation of violence is unsettling because, like Modthryth, she disables masculine identity in the process. Heroine though she is, Judith is also a threat to the masculine heroic order she exploits.

Violence which begins in the gaze ends in the inscription on bodies, as we have observed in Holofernes's plans to defile Judith "with stains."[23] Warfare is likewise conducted through the inscription of bodies toward the end of inscribing cultures, property, and possessions with the proprietorship of the victor. Judith's decapitation of Holofernes mimics just such an inscription, and there is no attempt in the poem to underplay or disguise the sheer violence of her action. Nor is there any question about the veiled sexuality of her violent act. The Old English text conflates acts of sexual and martial violence in a vivid enactment of what has only been suggested so far in the poem:

> Genam ða þone hæðenan mannan
> fæste be feaxe sinum,   teah hyne folmum wið hyre weard
> bysmerlice,   ond þone bealofullan
> listum alede,   laðne mannan,
> swa heo þæs unlædan   eaðost mihte
> wel gewealdan.   Sloh ða wundenlocc
> þone feondsceaðan   fagum mece,
> heteþoncolne,   þæt heo healfne forcearf
> þone sweoran him,   þæt he on swiman læg,
> druncen and dolhwund (98b–107).

> (She seized the heathen man
> firmly by his hair,   with her hands drew him to herself
> disgracefully,   and the wicked one
> skillfully laid down,   hateful man,
> so that she over the wretched one   most easily might
> completely gain power.   Then the woman with braided hair slew
> the hated enemy   with her shining sword,
> the hostile one,   so that she cut halfway
> through his neck   and he lay in a swoon
> drunk and wounded.)

Judith's manner of dragging Holofernes by the hair *bysmerlice* (disgracefully, or indecently) recalls his own plans to defile her (*besmitan*). Both Anglo-Saxon words connote defilement, staining with filth, and sexual disgrace. Further, as Olsen has noted, the word "wield" used to describe Judith's handling of Holofernes's body had connotations in Middle English of possessing, enjoying, or "swiving" a mistress.[24] The context of sexual violence lends this same word in Old English similar connotations, but with an important inversion of their application.

Hermann has drawn attention to the emphasis on hair in the decapitation scene—Judith's "braided locks," or "curly hair," and Holofernes's *feax*, or hair. It is significant, as Hermann also points out, that the only other use of *wundenlocc* to describe a woman also occurs in the context of suggested sexual violence in *Riddle 25*:

> Neþeð hwilum
> ful cyrtenu   ceorles dohtor,
> modwlonc meowle,   þæt heo on mec gripeð,
> ræseð mec on reodne,   reafað min heafod,
> fegeð mec on fæsten.   Feleþ sona
> mines gemotes,   seo þe mec nearwað,
> wif wundenlocc.[25]
>   (Sometimes ventures
> the beautiful   daughter of a peasant,
> courageous woman,   to grab hold of me,
> she attacks my red skin,   takes my head by force,
> confines me in a prison.)

Castration is the subtext of this well-known riddle of the onion. Its humor depends on our misreading of sexual violence for harvest, and "violent feminine appropriation of the talking penis" for the harmless plucking of a vegetable from its bed.[26]

The dragging of Holofernes by his hair not only makes legible his disgrace: it predicts the confusion of his military order and the defeat of his army. The excess which has marked his feast, his drinking, his desire, his self-indulgence, and even his voluptuousness proves his undoing, for excess obliterates the *legibility* of Holofernes's power and rank as a military leader by precipitating a confusion of categories. Gender and sexuality come to mark Holofernes, feminizing him and compromising his role as a leader. The notion of contamination—of defilement—is appropriate to the crisis figured in Holofernes's disgrace, for it suggests the breakdown and infiltration of boundaries. Holofernes's excess threatens his own power, role as leader, and his masculinity as well as the patriotism and loyalty identified with it. Suddenly, the excess—the armlets and rings (*beagum gehlæste, / hringum gerodene,* 36b–37a)—with which Judith has adorned herself to seduce Holofernes becomes transferred to Holofernes's body, and renders illegible the codes of power he has been so careful to establish.

The sexual violence of Judith's beheading takes the form of Holofernes's bodily inscription, which the text then proceeds to read. This inscription, in effect, renders Holofernes's body into a text, thereby feminizing it. When Holofernes collapses on his bed, he is reduced from signifying an "arrogant bestower of treasure" to a man "dazed with sins" (*ða niða geblonden*) after the drunken feast, to a body devoid of intelligence lying draped across its bed "in a swoon," and finally, to a "a foul trunk" (*se fula leap*). This headless trunk will prove to be the text of the Assyrians' defeat, while Judith will bear the grisly head home as a "token" of Bethulian victory. In both cases, bodily inscription serves as the text of war as well as of sexual violence; the one form of violence proves to be the subtext of the other. Just as Holofernes had intended his rape of Judith to symbolize his upcoming victory over the Bethulians, so now, his own defeat is signified through the foul trunk of his body and his severed head. While Judith will go on to "read" victory and divine sanction in Holofernes's head, the darker side of war and warrior culture—that is, their origins in sexual violence—is never absent from the poem.

A strangely humorous episode is generated by this crisis in which the codes of military rank, power, and victory are rewritten in gendered and sexualized terms. In the Assyrian camp the morning after the feast, Holofernes's retinue waits fretfully outside his tent for him to emerge. Not wishing to disturb him or even venturing to ask how things went with Judith, the men observe respect for the courtesies of male privilege even when the Bethulians are threatening to rout them. The rape of Judith takes precedence over this threat to their existence, as the group of retainers huddle together, coughing, gnashing their teeth, and making loud noises in an effort to awaken Holofernes without invading the scene of his supposed sexual conquest. When one lord finally does enter Holofernes's tent, he immediately reads in the leader's lifeless body the Assyrians' destruction at the hands of the Bethulians.

This scene renders dramatically the crisis of categories of rank and gender and the implications of that crisis for Assyrian society. The displacement of categories and the death of their leader causes temporary confusion, but more importantly, initiates that illegibility which Garber tracks inevitably to "collective and individual paranoia." When an As-

syrian lord discovers Holofernes's lifeless body, he indulges in a display
of grief which is usually marked feminine in Anglo-Saxon texts:

> He þa lungre gefeoll
> freorig to foldan,   ongan his feax teran,
> hreoh on mode,   ond his hrægl somod, . . . (280b–282)
> (He then suddenly fell
> filled with grief to the earth,   began to tear his hair,
> and his clothing together,   troubled in mind, . . .)

In this scene, Holofernes's own feminization at the hands of Judith
seems contagious, as the Assyrian warrior is thrown into feminine par-
oxysms of grief at the sight of Holofernes's lifeless trunk. His behavior
compares with those female mourners at Beowulf's funeral, who are
similarly distracted by grief.[27]

The crisis becomes complete with the fleeing of the Assyrian army.
It is not only the loss of their leader that triggers their "social and individual paranoia," but the breakdown of cultural legibility. The codes
of power have been destroyed and written over with those of gender and
sexuality. Suddenly, the Assyrian advantage—skill and military prow-
ess—is no longer meaningful. It has become meaningless—like the
body of Holofernes, reduced to a lifeless trunk. The sign, or *tacen*, has
been literally removed elsewhere, and as a result, the Assyrians lose
their heads.

Judith's return to the Bethulians is more sober and emphatic in its
signification. Instructing her servant to raise the head of Holofernes before the gates of the Bethulian camp, Judith gives a speech about the
glory that is signified (*getacnod*) by her victory over Holofernes. The
reversed sexual violence underlying her decapitation of Holofernes thus
becomes inscribed in her speech and the subsequent victory of the Bethulians. Instead of a routing of the masculine economy exploited by
Holofernes in Judith's victory, there is merely an inversion of its customary power relationships. The glory of the Bethulians is possible
through Judith's appropriation of the violence of the gaze and inscription, the two principles of violence in Holofernes's masculine culture.

While it is certainly significant that Judith is the agent of this appropriation, it is equally important that we notice how the same politics of
war based on sexual violence is operative in her appropriation. The
poem does not suggest a dismantling of Holofernes's vision of power
in Judith's reversal and spoiling of that vision. My point is that the

cultural politics of war, with all its affiliations with sexual violence, is insisted upon in the poem's portrayal of Judith's astounding victory. Although this ideological fashioning of the Judith story is not a critique, it does reflect an awareness of the intersection of two cultural practices.

What does it mean, then, for a woman to appropriate the masculine fantasies of rape and violence in her decapitation of Holofernes and her subsequent exhortation to battle? First, it exposes the interchangeability of war and sexual violence in Anglo-Saxon cultural codes. The one is not a displacement of the other, but its manifestation.[28] Klaus Theweleit theorizes that it is the "fear of dissolution through union with woman" that both collapses representations of woman with those of violence and forces men into homosocial relationships. The merging of sexual and military conquest thus serves, as Tania Modleski notes, to "conquer femininity both within and without."[29] The Anglo-Saxon *Judith* poem reveals the conjunction of sexual and military violence with fear of the feminine at the same time that it exposes the failure to "conquer femininity within and without." Thus, instead of resolving masculine fears of femininity, it forces a crisis in which these fears are made palpable by the feminization of Holofernes and his troops.

The poem's substitution of a woman in the role of authority succeeds chiefly in mocking the system represented by Holofernes and the Bethulians, but does not undermine it. The principle of inversion by which Judith-as-object is translated into Judith-as-subject of sexual violence and war preserves the power dynamics undergirding Assyrian warrior society in the first place. Judith's subjectivity depends on her objectification and the sexualization of military conquest. She is able to deploy Holofernes's system—to turn it against him—but without dismantling the disturbing categories her actions manifest. The masculine logic of violence is predicated on the gaze, its violence and objectification—and Judith manages to exploit this logic without disarming it.

Wulfstan's famous description of the rape of English women at the hands of the invading Danes in *Sermo Lupi ad Anglos* invokes this same complicity of the values and methods of war with the politics of sexual violence. The English men's shame in their battles with the Danes is represented by the rape of their women, including the gang rape of the wife of a thane, "while he looks on who considered himself proud and powerful and good enough before that happened."[30] The powerlessness of the gaze, in conjunction with sexual violence and the suggestion of violated property, is representative of the emotional and moral effects of war. Indeed, gender is inseparable from these effects and from the vision of a warrior culture as a whole. Sexual violence becomes emblematic of the violence done to property, pride, and the subjectivity enacted through the gaze.

If the Anglo-Saxons were not strangers to this intersection of the politics of war and sexual violence as it is construed in the *Judith* poem, neither are we. Uncensored reports from the Persian Gulf War in 1991 claimed that Navy bomber pilots were shown pornographic films before their bombing raids on Iraqi military and industrial complexes. The use of sexual violence in pornography to inspire military aggressiveness represents our own investment in the twin politics of war and sexual violence. Likewise, the male bombers' practice of giving the names of wives, girlfriends, and lovers to their bombs, which was proudly on display in the early days of the war, suggests the powerful confluence of sexual and warrior ideologies.

The masculine fear of "femininity within and without" found in the conjunction of idioms of sexual and martial conquest is also explicit in excerpts from a USAF fighter squadron's song book published in Joan Smith's study of *Misogynies*. A pamphlet that was meant to be circulated only among the group of pilots who composed it, *The Gamblers' Song Book* visualizes war as rape by feminizing and objectifying the enemy in a series of songs.[31] All of Holofernes's contempt for Judith is invoked in these songs, as well as the fear of women and sex underlying that contempt.

The celebration of violence toward women can likewise be found in Naval Academy practices and in the Navy's Tailhook scandal, where misogyny becomes a form of ritual practice.[32] The homosocial bonds of the feasting community, which provided the context for Holofernes's intended rape of Judith, are created through coded violence toward women, whether in pilot's songs, naval academy marching chants, or Tailhook traditions. Pornography becomes the chief mode of experiencing war, and it is unsparing in its contempt for, and violence toward, women.

"The visual is *essentially* pornographic, which is to say that it has its end in rapt, mindless fascination," writes Fredric Jameson in his recent study of film, *Signatures of the Visible*.[33] While Jameson's comment is about contemporary film culture, it might also explain the intersection of ideologies of war and sexual violence in the Old English *Judith*. For it is Holofernes who renders the world he rules a pornographic one through his exploitation of the masculine gaze. In objectifying his retainers as well as marking the Bethulians for conquest, Holofernes treats this world as a body to be stared at, and hence, mastered. He seeks out bodies through rape and conquest to bear the signature of his gaze and his power.[34] While his own pornographic vision recoils on him when Judith decapitates him, the essential complicity of that vision with the ideology of war is never erased from the poem. With the gory head of Holofernes raised by her attendant as a visual prop, Judith incorporates the pornographic gaze into her own vision of victory. Even if a woman is now the agent of violence and sexual assault, the fantasy of Holofernes—to defile and stain a woman—remains intact. The woman about to be defiled always haunts the heroic speeches of warriors, the brave deeds of Judith and her army, and acts of God in the struggles between nations.

Intersecting the categories of gender and class (or military rank) reveals the deeper cultural pairing of sexual violence and war. The easy slippage from Holofernes's war feast to his plan to defile Judith is reversed, though not subverted, by Judith's decapitation of him. Holofernes's emblem of military rank and power—his veiled bed and invisible voice/body—employs gender as a category of meaning. The twin categories of the masculine and the feminine undergird the larger structures of rank (leader/subordinate) and of war (victors/conquered and sexual violence/military violence). When these categories are crossed or undone, as they are when Judith decapitates Holofernes, a crisis of individual and collective identity ensues.

We have seen in Wulfstan's remarks on the Anglo-Saxon demoralization at the hands of the Danes in his *Sermo Lupi ad Anglos* how closely tied were cultural identities with these categories. Sexual violence, the feminization of Anglo-Saxons, and loss of class boundaries all represent for Wulfstan the deeper crisis of collective identity at issue in the Danish attacks. What Wulfstan laments is the loss of cultural legibility in the codes of gender and class in particular, and what he appeals to is a return to a legibility lost during the war with the Danes, and with it, a restoration of cultural identity and morality. The Old English *Judith* offers an interesting commentary on Wulfstan's vision of a restored Anglo-Saxon community. Instead of using Wulfstan to read *Judith,* we might learn something about ourselves and Anglo-Saxon culture by reading *Judith* against Wulfstan's sermon. In the Old English poem, we can learn to read Wulfstan's fears in terms of the cultural categories which make them legible to us, and to see that the origins of these fears are, in part, of our own creation.

Notes

1. Marjorie Garber, *Vested Interests: Cross-Dressing and Cultural Anxiety* (New York: Routledge, 1992), 25. Garber is specifically addressing the implications of dress codes for cultures beyond the social and economic spheres for which they are specifically designed. In this chapter I am interested in the ways in which the Old English *Judith* incorporates such "cultural legislation" in its codes of gender and rank and its investigation of the collective paranoia which results and which is implicated in the war between the Assyrians and Bethulians.

2. See her introduction, *Vested Interests,* 16–17. Binarism remains the abiding structural principle of the interdependence of categories in Garber's analysis. Thus, a crisis in one area, such as gender, "indicates a *category crisis elsewhere,* an irresolvable conflict or epistemological crux that destabilizes comfortable binarity, and displaces the resulting discomfort onto a figure that already inhabits, indeed incarnates, the margin" (17). For another analysis of the mutual reinforcing function of cultural binarisms, see Eve Kosofsky Sedgwick, *The Epistemology of the Closet* (Berkeley: University of California Press, 1991), 1–66, esp. 11–12.

3. Garber, too, suggests the interchangeability of the categories of class and rank, calling the first the "civilian counterpart" of rank, *Vested Interests,* 25.

4. The first interpretation is Bernard F. Huppé's, *The Web of Words* (Albany: State University of New York Press, 1970), 148. Among those who read the poem as a celebration of Judith's chastity, even though no mention is made of it, are R. E. Woolf, "The Lost Opening to the *Judith,*" *MLR* 50 (1955): 171; Stanley B. Greenfield, *A Critical History of Old English Literature* (New York, 1965), 165. Scholars who read Judith allegorically as a figure of the Church include Jane Chance, *Woman as Hero in Old English Literature* (Syracuse: Syracuse University Press, 1986), 37; and John P. Hermann, *Allegories of War: Language and Violence in Old English Poetry* (Ann Arbor: University of Michigan Press, 1989), 194–98. Hermann's analysis departs from the usual exegesis of the poem by drawing upon psychoanalysis to argue that the poem allegorizes the formation of the Christian subject and the "disciplining" of desire for the mother in *Ecclesia.* For a summary of the various readings of the poem, see David Chamberlain, "*Judith:* A Fragmentary and Political Poem," in *Anglo-Saxon Poetry: Essays In Appreciation,* ed. Lewis E. Nicholson and Dolores Warwick Frese (Notre Dame: University of Notre Dame Press, 1975), 135–36 and 154–57; Hermann, *Allegories of War,* 181–84 and 187–88; and Alexandra Hennessey Olsen, "Inversion and Political Purpose in the Old English *Judith,*" *English Studies* 63 (1982): 289–90.

5. Quoted in Chamberlain, "*Judith:* A Fragmentary and Political Poem," 144. Both Chamberlain and Olsen also point to the Chronicle and the sermons of Ælfric for descriptions of conditions under Danish siege as a cultural context for the poem, 158–59 and 292–93, respectively.

6. Hermann objects to the assumed incompatibility of these two kinds of reading in most critics' approaches, averring that "there is no good reason why

allegorical dimensions cannot coexist with sexual violence in *Judith*" (187). However, his statement changes the terms of the discussion, unconsciously, I think, from one of politics and allegory to one of sexual violence and allegory. Hermann's own analysis, while it is meant to overcome the mutual exclusivity of the two kinds of reading, ends up being mainly an allegorical one with psychoanalytic features.

7. For an excellent critique of source study and exegetical criticism in Old English scholarship, see Allen J. Frantzen, *Desire for Origins: New Language, Old English, and Teaching the Tradition* (New Brunswick: Rutgers University Press, 1990), 79–95; in Middle English studies, see Lee Patterson, *Negotiating the Past: The Historical Understanding of Medieval Literature* (Madison: University of Wisconsin Press, 1987), 26–39.

8. In addition to Frantzen's critique of this approach (see n. 7), Clare A. Lees points out the self-perpetuating project of much source study, and argues for alternative models for studying textual relationships using Hans Robert Jauss's reception theory and Michel Foucault's notion of archaeology, "Working with Patristic Sources," in *Speaking Two Languages: Traditional Disciplines and Contemporary Theory in Medieval Studies*, ed. Allen J. Frantzen (Albany: State University of New York Press, 1991), 157–80.

9. I am summarizing David Chamberlain's method in his reconstruction of the Old English poem, "*Judith:* A Fragmentary and Political Poem," 145.

10. Patterson critiques various scholarly efforts to historicize texts by reconstructing their contexts and foreclosing their interpretation at the same time. Among those schools of criticism guilty of such preemptive strategies, Patterson counts the nineteenth-century historicists, the Exegetical critics, and Marxist scholars. See *Negotiating the Past: The Historical Understanding of Medieval Literature* (Madison: University of Wisconsin Press, 1987), 13–18, 26–39, and 48–52.

11. Burton Raffel, "*Judith:* Hypermetricity and Rhetoric," in *Anglo-Saxon Poetry: Essays in Appreciation,* ed. Lewis E. Nicholson and Dolores Warwick Frese (Notre Dame: University of Notre Dame Press, 1975), 124. Raffel goes on to talk about the poem's hypermetricity, but his opening remarks seem not to be limited to its prosodic peculiarities. In *Allegories of War* Hermann alludes to Raffel's discomfort and confesses that "my own reaction to the poem is characterized by a similar sense of disquiet" (186). In neither case, however, is this disquiet investigated; instead, it is put aside in favor of psychoanalytic allegorizing and hypermetric analysis—moves which are, perhaps, as much symptoms of the disquiet as they are modes of academic inquiry.

12. This argument about Judith's strength is not a particularly feminist one, since it may be found in just about every biblical commentary and most scholarly evaluations of the Anglo-Saxon figure. It is also not feminist because it relies on the unexamined assumption that women in Anglo-Saxon culture were usually represented as passive, and that a strong woman such as Judith therefore approached the male ideals of heroism. This binarism is mostly a creation of Anglo-Saxon scholars, but it is largely assumed to be a fact of Anglo-Saxon culture. For a critique of this view, see Gillian R. Overing, Helen T. Bennett, and Clare A. Lees, "Gender and Power: Feminism in Old English Studies," *Medieval Feminist Newsletter* 10 (1990): 15–20.

13. _Language, Sign, and Gender in_ Beowulf (Carbondale: Southern Illinois University Press, 1990), 92–93.

14. Beowulf _and_ Judith, ed. Elliott Van Kirk Dobbie (New York: Columbia University Press, 1953), 21b–27. All subsequent quotations will be made from this edition and will be cited in the text. Translations into English are my own.

15. Hermann also calls Holofernes a "male parody," and contrasts his depiction with "the transcendent male principle of divine patriarchy" which guides Judith, _Allegories of War,_ 187.

16. "Ðær wæs hæleþa hleahtor, hlyn swynsode, / word wæron wynsume (611–12). The bench-noise (_bencsweg,_ 1161) of the Danish and Geatish warriors is one of joy, however, rather than drunkenness. One wonders if the two sounds were distinguishable to the "sons of men" who could hear them miles away.

17. There is a distinct similarity between the two feasts in _Judith_ and _Vainglory_ because of the inarticulate sounds of drunken excess and the suggestions of pride in both. See _Vainglory,_ in _The Exeter Book,_ ed. George Philip Krapp and Elliott Van Kirk Dobbie, Anglo-Saxon Poetic Records III (New York: Columbia University Press, 1936), 9–29.

18. Eve Kosofsky Sedgwick, _Between Men: English Literature and Male Homosocial Desire_ (New York: Columbia University Press, 1985), 1. Sedgwick distinguishes this homosociality from homosexuality, claiming that the former is the "social force" structuring men's relationships. She argues that patriarchy enforces a discontinuity between the two, so that the social relationships among men are radically differentiated from homosexual relationships. See her discussion, 1–5.

19. Overing draws upon the categories of speech-acts outlined by J. L. Austin and John Searle to demonstrate how Wealhtheow's speeches differ significantly from those of the hero, _Language, Sign, and Gender in_ Beowulf, 92–107.

20. See Luce Irigaray, _Speculum of the Other Woman,_ trans. Gillian C. Gill (Ithaca: Cornell University Press, 1985), 13–146.

21. In this formulation, Moi summarizes Freud's notion of the gaze as it relates to power and mastery, _Sexual/Textual Politics: Feminist Literary Theory_ (London: Methuen, 1985), 180n.8.

22. Jane Chance places Judith in the company of Juliana and Elene, two other "fighting women saints," _Woman as Hero in Old English Literature,_ 31–52. Olsen joins David K. Crowne and Donald K. Fry in viewing Judith, along with Beowulf, Hnæf, Andreas, and Constantine, as a type of the Hero on the Beach; see Olsen "Inversion and Political Purpose in the Old English _Judith,_" 289–90. My comparison of Judith to Modthryth is indebted to Gillian R. Overing's very interesting analysis of the latter, _Language, Sign, and Gender in_ Beowulf, 101–108.

23. I am borrowing Overing's discussion of violence as it is theorized in the works of Gilles Deleuze and Felix Guattari. See _Language, Sign, and Gender in_ Beowulf, 90–94.

24. Olsen draws upon E. Talbot Donaldson's analysis of the Middle English word, "Inversion and Political Purpose in the Old English _Judith,_" 291n.

25. *The Exeter Book*, 193. For Hermann's discussion of this riddle, see *Allegories of War*, 191–92.

26. I am borrowing Hermann's language here, *Allegories of War*, 192.

27. For a study of the female mourner in Anglo-Saxon and Old Norse culture, see Helen T. Bennett, "The Female Mourner at Beowulf's Funeral: Filling in the Blanks/Hearing the Spaces" *Exemplaria* 4 (Spring 1992): 35–50.

28. My argument here is indebted to Tania Modleski's discussion of the war film in *Feminism without Women: Culture and Criticism in a 'Postfeminist' Age* (New York: Routledge, 1991), 61–75, particularly p. 62.

29. Klaus Theweleit, *Male Fantasies*, vol. 1: *Floods, Bodies, History*, trans. Stephen Conway with Erica Carter and Chris Turner (Minneapolis: University of Minnesota Press, 1987), 50; Modleski, *Feminism without Women*, 63.

30. ". . . þær he on locað, þe læt hine sylfne rancne and ricne and genoh godne ær þæt gewurde," *Sermo Lupi ad Anglos* in *The Homilies of Wulfstan*, ed. Dorothy Bethurum (Oxford, 1957), 264.

31. Joan Smith, *Misogynies* (London: Faber, 1989), 99–111. Smith quotes examples of the feminization of the enemy in sexual terms: "Leaving the orbit our pits start to sweat / We'll asshole those fuckers and that's a sure bet / Burn all those Ruskies [*sic*] and cover 'em with dirt / That's why we love sitting Victor Alert" (100). The enemy is figured in the *Gamblers' Song Book* as "a slant-eyed bitch" needing to be raped and as "a dead whore by the road side" (102, 103).

32. For a discussion of Naval Academy misogynistic practices and their relationship to the Tailhook scandal, see Carol Burke, "Dames at Sea," *The New Republic* (Aug. 17 and 24, 1992): 16–20.

33. *Signatures of the Visible* (New York: Routledge, 1990), 1.

34. I am borrowing Jameson's idea that pornographic films "ask us to stare at the world as though it were a naked body," *Signatures of the Visible*, 1.

Wonfeax wale

IDEOLOGY AND FIGURATION IN THE SEXUAL RIDDLES OF THE EXETER BOOK

❋ ❋ ❋

John W. Tanke

Although the Exeter Book riddles have never been accorded a central place in Anglo-Saxon literary culture, scholars have consistently seen in them a set of unique rhetorical and epistemological virtues not shared by more widely studied genres of Old English literature. Frederick Tupper, the first important American student of the riddles, describes them this way: "Nothing human is deemed too high or low for treatment, and all phases of Old English existence are revealed in these poems."[1] Charles Kennedy writes: "By their range and detailed vividness, the *Riddles* supplement the pictures of Old English culture derived from the narrative poems,"[2] while Fred Robinson suggests that they "reveal quirks and moods of the Anglo-Saxons quite unlike anything we find in their other poetry."[3] Recently, Seth Lerer has argued that the Exeter Book riddles are "essentially an epistemological poetry" composed by and for "the literate elite" in Anglo-Saxon society.[4] He argues that "the power of literacy, here, is the power to classify," and that "by creating a system of classification the writer or compiler (of encyclopedic riddle collections) exerts a control over the world."[5] Lerer's conclusion is essentially the same as Tupper's: as a genre of "catalogue poetry," the Exeter Book riddle corpus "brings the scope of individual experience together into a complete and readable whole."[6] Whereas Tupper praises the riddles for revealing the low as well as the high points of what he calls "Old English existence," Kennedy and Robinson—perhaps in response to the "low points"—see them as a literary-historical supplement to the canon of Old English texts. For all of these scholars, however, the Exeter Book riddles possess extraordinary powers of revelation: they provide us with a window onto the Anglo-Saxon

world, revealing much which the rest of the literature conceals. This
assessment is remarkable since it is, after all, riddles which are in question, texts which would seem to have no small stake in concealing what
they promise to reveal.

The fact that the corpus of Old English riddles contains many which
deal with sexuality (the so-called double-entendre riddles in particular)
certainly attests to the largely unprecedented nature of its content. But
is this content so easily revealed? Can we say, following Lerer, that the
scope of *sexual experience* is here brought together "into a complete
and readable whole"? Do the sexual riddles deploy classifications
whose aim is simply to reveal the pre-existing "reality" of sexual experience in Anglo-Saxon England, or do these classifications exert an
ideological force whose aim is not simply to represent but to construct
a sexual order? I will argue that the latter thesis is more productive
since it is by no means clear that the community which composed these
riddles had any great interest in what we call "individuals." The sexual
riddles in the Exeter Book feature a variety of subjects (men and
women, nobles and slaves, English and Welsh), whose symbolic differences are exploited in enigmatic ways.

The issue of social class has figured prominently in generic discussions of the sexual riddles. Several scholars have claimed that these poems were composed either for or about the "lower classes" of Anglo-
Saxon society. This thesis is supported by the tacit assumption of a
natural association between sexual representation and the lower class,
and although it has been largely discredited, it still haunts the discussion of sexual rhetoric in the riddles. In order to establish a critical context for a reading of Riddle 12 at the end of this chapter, I will be
focusing in particular on scholarly discussion of the *wonfeax wale*
(dark-haired servant woman) who appears in Riddles 12 and 52. The
word *wale* (female servant and/or Welshwoman), like its masculine
counterpart *wealh* (male servant and/or Welshman), is especially interesting insofar as it raises questions of class, gender, and ethnicity.

Another issue of generic classification I will be discussing involves
both the rhetorical structure of the double-entendre riddle and the
social-psychological framework within which the posing and solving of
such a riddle is assumed to take place. Since the double-entendre riddle
encrypts both a sexual and a non-sexual content, solving it demands
that the reader-listener take a position *vis-à-vis* these two semantic
worlds. Scholars have presupposed that the non-sexual solution is both
the "true" and "harmless" solution, while the sexual solution is both

"false" and in some sense "harmful." In this view, the riddle poser seeks to elicit a sexual rather than a non-sexual solution, in order to expose the solver's knowledge of, and desire for, sexual representation.

Problems of class, gender, and ethnicity on the one hand and the ideological dimensions of the double-entendre riddle on the other intersect dramatically in Exeter Book Riddle 12. Unanimously solved as "ox/leather," this riddle explores the relations between a variety of classifications: nature and culture, master and servant, male and female, to name but a few. It also raises problems of classification of another kind: since only the second half of the riddle—in which the *wonfeax wale* appears—uses sexually suggestive language, it does not fit the mold of the typical double entendre. The riddle breaks this mold in another way as well: whereas the majority of sexual *personae* who appear in the double-entendre riddles are presented in an ethically neutral or even positive light, the "dark-haired servant woman" is held up for contempt. Solving this riddle demands that we account for the apparently gratuitous description of her as *dol druncmennen*, a phrase which may mean "foolish drunken slave-woman."

The Rhetoric of the Lower Class

Criticism has consistently associated the sexual riddles of the Exeter Book with the lower classes of Anglo-Saxon England. Underwriting this association is, of course, the widely accepted distinction between "literary" and "popular" riddles. While demonstrating considerable sensitivity to the difficulties which such a distinction entails for the Exeter Book collection in general, Frederick Tupper felt himself on firm ground when discussing the sub-group of sexual riddles. The "puzzles of double meaning and coarse suggestion," he asserts, "in their form and substance, are so evidently popular products as to suggest that the poet has yielded in large measure to the collector."[7] This view led him to remark mistakenly that the sexual riddles feature predominantly lower-class characters. On the status of the notorious *superne secg* or "southern man" of Riddle 62, who seems to be engaged in anal intercourse, Tupper notes: he "is obviously in the same class as 'the dark-haired Welsh,' the churls and esnes, often people of un-English origin, who figure in these folk-products."[8] As this moment reveals, the association of sexual representation with the lower class often has a racial or ethnic component. The association of foreign slaves (*wealh* can mean "Welsh" and/or "slave"), servants in general (*esne* means "male servant"), and "churls" (*ceorlas* were by definition free and most were certainly English) with "the folk" is remarkable: evidently to be truly English one had to be fairly well off indeed.

Ann Harleman Stewart has corrected Tupper's assertions about class, pointing out that of the fifteen class-specific terms in the corpus of sexual riddles only four are lower-class. She concludes: "Here we have the opposite of what would be expected, as far as class distinctions are concerned," and "the co-occurrence of sexual slang and bawdily direct imagery with references to upper-class participants is hard to interpret."[9] That Stewart expected her survey to confirm Tupper's claim reveals that she, too, finds the association of sexual riddles with the lower class a natural one. The association of sexual imagery with upper-class characters is "hard to interpret," whereas presumably the association of such imagery with lower-class figures, being natural and self-explanatory, demands no interpretation.

Let us now turn to the problem of the *wonfeax wale* or "dark-haired servant-woman" in Riddle 12. As I noted above, the sparsely attested Old English word *wale*, together with its more common masculine counterpart *wealh*, can mean either "Welsh person" or "slave." In a long and fascinating note to the *wonfeax wale* of Riddle 12, Tupper asserts:

> That *Wealh* is used in the meaning of "servus" is naturally explained by the position which the old inhabitants of Britain held under the Anglo-Saxon rule. . . . *Wealh* was applied, without regard to origin, to bond-men who were, however, largely of Celtic or Pre-Celtic blood.[10]

We learn two somewhat contradictory things here: (1) that *wealh* signified the servant class "without regard to origin," and (2) that these people were nonetheless Celts. Tupper's anxiety with *wealh* seems to have to do with the artificiality, the impropriety of this word's two meanings: he is bothered (with reason, it seems to me) by the possibility that a non-Celt might be called a Celt, and that a freeman might be called a slave. He attempts to solve this enigma by pointing out that, after all, most slaves were Celts (a thesis which is certainly open to question, especially in view of the ambiguity of the word *wealh*). This desire to restore to language some stability of reference, by eliding semantic difference, parallels the desire to efface the difference in Anglo-

Saxon society (or, from another perspective, to enforce it). The violence which makes a slave out of a Welsh person parallels the violence
in language which makes one say "slave" when one means "Welsh"
and "Welsh" when one means "slave." *Wealh* is one of those enigmatic words whose usage dramatizes its meaning: it is a word from
whose otherness there is no escape.

In a more recent consideration of the word *wealh* in the riddles, Margaret Lindsay Faull argues that its two meanings should be kept separate. She pays particular attention to a passage in Riddle 12 in which
the riddle subject (at this point an ox) says:

> Gif me feorh losað,   fæste binde
> swearte wealas,   hwilum sellan men.[11]
>
> (3–4)

(If life leaves me, I bind fast dark *wealas*, sometimes better men.)

Of this passage and the terms *wealh/wale* in general, Faull comments:

> Baum translates *wealas* as "Welsh" and *wale* as "Welsh girl" but he is
> probably mistaken. Oxhide would naturally have been used to bind
> slaves in contrast to *sellan men*: racial prejudice might have led to En-
> glish men being regarded as "better" than the *Wealas* but there is no
> indication that the comparison here is with English people, especially as
> Aldhelm's Latin version, on which Riddle xii was based, has the neutral
> *Nexibus horrendis homines constringere possum* without racial implica-
> tions. Nor are the dark *wealas* of the first two riddles likely to be any-
> thing more than ordinary female slaves, although *feorran broht* in Riddle
> xii might suggest that this *wealh* had come from Wales, which before the
> Norse invasions supplied the Anglo-Saxons with slaves taken in border
> raids. The swarthiness and dark hair of the slaves do not prove, as F.
> Tupper believes, that there was a large Celtic proportion in the slave
> population as all Anglo-Saxons were not fair either. The Germanic peo-
> ples may have preferred fair hair and so ascribed the opposite charac-
> teristics to the lowest ranks of society.[12]

Faull's argument that *wealas* and *wale* refer not to race but to class is
open to serious objection. For one thing, the Latin "source" she ad-
duces for Riddle 12 is at best an analogue. Eleven of Riddle 12's fifteen
lines find no parallel whatsoever in Aldhelm's much shorter riddle; in
no way can the Latin text be termed a "version" of the Old English.

More importantly, the "neutrality" of the Latin *homines* is precisely what distinguishes Aldhelm's riddle from Riddle 12, with its opposition between dark *wealas* and "better men." While Faull is correct to point out that *wealh* need not mean "Welsh," she neglects to mention that it need not mean simply "slave" either. The same problem affects her discussion of epithets such as "dark-haired," which Tupper reads as having racial connotations. If the Anglo-Saxons were free to stereotype slaves as dark-haired, what prevented them from stereotyping Celts this way?

Discussions of social class in the riddles often have a gender component as well. In the same note to *wonfeax wale*, Tupper cites a comment about women-servants from F. York Powell, one of the contributors to H. D. Traill's *Social England*, published in 1902. As a fuller account of his comment reveals (Tupper quotes only the second sentence in what follows), Powell's mention of women-servants is tied to a more general reflection on the class structure of Anglo-Saxon England:

> The same kind of division of classes seems to have prevailed from as far back as we get evidence as to the condition of an English village down to the present day; of course with slightly differing legal rights. Thus in early times the women-servants and menials about the yeoman's or gentleman's house were absolute slaves, and were bought and sold as cattle.[13]

It is remarkable by itself that Anglo-Saxon and Edwardian England should be thus equated, but it is even more remarkable that this equation should be based on "women-servants and menials about the yeoman's or gentleman's house." Since Powell makes no explicit reference to gender in his discussion, this comment gratuitously implies a "privileged" relation between femininity and servitude. If nothing else, one has to admire the honesty of the implication that, although they now possess "slightly differing legal rights," such persons are still, in Powell's day, "bought and sold like cattle."

In Tupper's gloss on the term *wealh*, we saw how the improper association of its two meanings, "Welsh" and "slave," is naturalized, and in Powell's comments on class, how the institution of the domestic woman-servant is characterized as an unchanging, thus natural, part of English society. Agop Hacikyan provides an especially striking instance of this tendency to naturalize social classifications. Here, too, the issue

of gender surfaces more or less gratuitously in a discussion ostensibly
restricted to social class:

> Besides the ideas of loyalty to one's lord and reward for bravery among
> the ruling powers of the nation, there is likewise the sense of responsi-
> bility and care with which the peasant or the slave performs his duties.
> There seems to be a complete harmony amidst the multi-echeloned hi-
> erarchical system of early English society; the Welsh woman, the slave,
> serves her master in utmost obedience, and he, in return, provides, and
> praises her good service.[14]

The riddles provide no evidence whatsoever to support these assertions. A (possibly Welsh) woman-servant occurs in two riddles, 12
and 52, and neither of these has anything explicit to say about the relations between servant and master, let alone the idea that *she* serves
him "in utmost obedience," while he, "in return, provides, and praises
her good service."

Liberation and Enslavement: Theory of the Double Entendre

A strictly philological approach to the politics of sexual representation in the riddles is taken by Bogislav von Lindheim. He suggests that
the twin ideologies of Christianity and Germanic heroism were responsible for a censorship of colloquial speech in Old English literature:

> Both (ideologies) strove to suppress the vigorous and coarser features of
> ordinary colloquial speech. . . . Unrestrained growth of free colloquial
> speech never had much of a chance in Anglo-Saxon times owing to the
> peculiar political and social organisation of the country.[15]

By "vigorous and coarser features of ordinary colloquial speech," von
Lindheim means words denoting sexual excitement and/or parts of the
human body, examples being *wlanc* and *gal* (lustful), *neb* (nose, face),
þyrel (hole), and *wamb* (belly, womb, receptacle). Since such words
occur more frequently in the Exeter Book riddles than elsewhere, he
concludes that the riddle genre acted as a refuge for Old English
colloquialisms.[16] The essential ambiguity of riddles, he reasons, "allowed the admission of a vulgar strain, disguised under the cloak of
harmless and edifying solutions."[17] This argument is noteworthy not

because ideology is understood to censor sexual language, but because these two terms are opposed to begin with: before ideology succeeds in suppressing it, sexual language is non-ideological, that is, "free."

The problematic relations between ideology and sexual language become strikingly evident if we look to what has become the accepted social-psychological framework used to interpret the "game" of the Old English double entendre. As Craig Williamson writes:

> The erotic double-entendre riddle has both a prim and a pornographic solution. This places the potential solver in a double bind: either his naiveté or his salacious imagination is bound to be exposed.[18]

And further:

> One might speculate that the original game consisted of inducing the riddle-solver to guess the "wrong" solution, that is the anatomical one, in order to offer him the "plain" solution and proof of his salacious imagination.[19]

Along the same lines Reinhard Gleissner states:

> The obscene riddle of double entendre functions as a piece of wit insofar as the riddle solver is practically always a dupe. If he arrives at the "correct," i.e., harmless, solution, he is laughed at for his naive sensibility. If, as the riddle poser intends, he falls for the "incorrect," i.e., indecent, obscene solution, one laughs at him for his naive fantasy, and presents him with the "correct," i.e., harmless solution.[20]

And further:

> Double-entendre riddles rather obviously lead the hearer to an erotic solution in order then to expose him with the "actual"decent solution.[21]

In order to solve a double-entendre riddle, an artificial semantic hierarchy must be established: one of the two subjects simultaneously represented must be credited as "real" and the other as unreal. Gleissner and Williamson both assume that the sexual solution of a double-entendre riddle is the wrong solution, while the non-sexual solution is the right one. And while each scholar affirms the doubleness of the "double bind," each clearly prefers one outcome: the "original" purpose of the riddle is for the riddler to lure the solver to propose the sexual solution, in order then to expose his salacious imagination. The riddle accomplishes this exposure by means of two possible significations, one "harmless," the other, by implication, "harmful." The riddler aims to harm by luring the solver to choose the "false" solution, thereby exposing a desire for and/or knowledge of sexual representation. Criticism has been unanimous in characterizing the double-entendre riddle in Old English as a game of rhetorical seduction and censorship.[22]

Gleissner has gone further than most scholars in his attempt to theorize the double entendre, expanding the scope of his analysis from the intersubjective dynamics of riddle poser and riddle solver to the dynamic relation which obtains between the obscene joke on the one hand and cultural prohibitions on sexual representation on the other:

> The double-entendre riddle's function as a joke also allows one to resist the prick of a sexual tabu which is felt to be burdensome. The tabu and the law on which it is founded are attacked and injured by the joke, whereby the laughter elicited by the joke has a liberating effect. Yet the deviation from the law caused by the joke never goes so far as to do away with the law entirely. The joke, in order to be understood and in order to function properly, needs the law, which it opposes and assaults. On the other hand, there must already be a certain detachment from the established law, which allows it to be ridiculed.[23]

At first glance this dynamic of the law and the sexual joke seems rather obviously appropriate. The law "binds" the subject, and the subject, thus oppressed, seeks to free him- or herself from the law by means of the double-entendre riddle as joke. But what kind of laughter is generated when the riddler's aim is to ridicule the solver's naiveté or salacious imagination? If one accepts that it is the riddler's aim to cause the solver to expose his/her desire for a sexual solution and then to reject the validity of that solution, thereby ridiculing the solver, then it becomes clear that the riddle aims not to do battle with the law, but rather to exploit and thereby affirm it. Paradoxically, sexual language is liberated only to the extent that the harmless solution in turn liberates the solver from the need to identify the representation as sexual.

This model will appear even more problematic when we attempt to apply it to Riddle 12 and the *wonfeax wale*. If the laughter elicited by the sexual joke has a "liberating" effect, what do we make of the fact that the figure whose representation elicits this laughter is herself a slave? That the figure used to ridicule the law is herself ridiculed? If the double entendre facilitates a liberation of repression, does this liberation also depend on the enslavement of the "dark-haired servant woman"? If so, then the riddlers' ostensibly antagonistic relation to the law is again called into question, for they would seem to be invoking the law even as they ostensibly flout it. In fact, our reading of Riddle 12 will suggest that their interest is not to flout the law at all, but rather to get the *wale* to flout it for them.

Another problem with this theory of the double-entendre riddle is its effacement of sexual difference. Recall that in Freud's theory of *die Zote* or dirty joke the gender of the participants is a matter of crucial importance: both the teller of the joke and its addressee, the subject whose sexual repression is momentarily alleviated, are assumed to be male. The figure represented in the joke, whose sexuality is exposed, is assumed to be female. Masculine desire manifests itself here as an aggressive projection of lack onto women.[24] Freud's model can help us to appreciate that while the sexual joke may do battle with the law against sexual representation, it is quite capable of celebrating and reaffirming the "law" of sexual difference.

Finally, what does the interactive relationship between riddle poser and riddle solver, as outlined by Gleissner and Williamson, say about the relation between revelation and concealment in riddle rhetoric? To pass this test of sexual representation and reaffirm their adherence to the symbolic laws of the riddle community, solvers must resist the poser's desire that they expose their knowledge of sexuality. Solving a double-entendre riddle involves the concealment of its sexual solution.

Sexual Representation in the Riddles: Problems of Classification

The foregoing discussion obviously assumes that sexual rhetoric in the Exeter Book falls within the province of the double-entendre riddle. This assumption suggests to the student unfamiliar with the Exeter Book riddle corpus that all of those riddles which have a sexual content are double-entendre riddles, and suggests to novice and specialist alike that the double-entendre riddles are the best or most exemplary riddles dealing with sexuality. It is important to realize, however, that the first implication is incorrect: of the fourteen riddles which deal in one way or another with sexuality, only seven (25, 37, 44, 45, 54, 61, 62) fit the definition of the "classic" double-entendre riddle, in which there is an ambiguity, sustained throughout the text, between a sexual and a non-sexual content. We are left with another seven riddles (12, 20, 42, 46, 63, 77, 91) which treat sexual subjects, but for one reason or another do not fit the double-entendre genre. Of these, only Riddles 20 and 42 have met with much discussion.[25]

Before discussing Riddle 12, one of those riddles which does not fit the double-entendre matrix, and in order to facilitate a comparison, let us briefly examine the rhetoric of one "classical" double-entendre riddle: Riddle 25. Every detail which the riddle subject uses to describe itself points simultaneously to two possible solutions—onion and penis:

> Ic eom wunderlicu wiht,   wifum on hyhte,
> neahbuendum nyt;   nængum sceþþe
> burgsittendra,   nymþe bonan anum.
> Staþol min is steapheah,   stonde ic on bedde,
> neoþan ruh nathwær.   Neþeð hwilum
> ful cyrtenu   ceorles dohtor,
> modwlonc meowle,   þæt heo on mec gripeð,
> ræseð mec on reodne,   reafað min heafod,
> fegeð mec on fæsten.   Feleþ sona
> mines gemotes,   seo þe mec nearwað,
> wif wundenlocc.   Wæt bið þæt eage.

(I am a marvelous creature: a joy to women, useful to neighbors. I harm no citizen except my slayer alone. My station is very high, I stand on a bed, rough somewhere beneath. At times a very becoming churl's daughter, proud (or: lusty) woman, ventures forth, so that she grasps me, rushes upon my redness, plunders my head, fits me in a secure place. She who approaches me, curly-haired woman, feels our meeting immediately: wet is the eye.)

This riddle has become one of the best-loved double-entendre riddles in the Exeter Book. As Craig Williamson states: "Tupper classifies the riddle as 'obscene,' but surely some will find more pleasure in it than lack of propriety."[26] A part of this riddle's rustic charm comes from the numerous positive epithets applied to the onion-picking woman: she is described as *cyrtenu,* an adjective meaning "becoming" derived from the Latin root of modern English "courtly," *modwlonc* (proud, lusty), and *wundenlocc* (curly-haired). Moreover, as a *ceorles dohtor* (churl's daughter), she neither surprises us in her sexual activity (as she might were she described as noble) nor invites us to look down on her (as she might if she were a slave). The violence she inflicts on the masculine riddle subject is avenged by the tear she is made to yield, and the ejaculate she receives. Stewart sums up the favorable impression this riddle has made by noting: "It is comic rather than crude, ribald rather than lascivious, with a sort of affectionate ridicule that is the opposite of prurience."[27] In the notes to Williamson's translation we can find another rationale for its "harmlessness": "The phallic onion links the green world with the world of human sexuality. Nature is charged with human metaphor; passion is charted with natural myth."[28] The key word here is "nature": natural, heterosexual activity is likened to onion-picking. As we will see in a moment, however, it is the realm of culture (in every sense of the word) that is represented as sexually charged in Riddle 12.

Slavery and Sexuality: A Reading of Riddle 12

If the riddles are a marginal genre in Old English, and the subset of double-entendre riddles is still more marginal, Riddle 12 must be among the most marginal Old English texts of all. Apparently, only lines 7b–13a involving the *wonfeax wale* (dark-haired servant-woman) can be read as a double entendre. For this reason, and perhaps also because its rhetoric is far from "harmless," Riddle 12 has never received what could be called an interpretation. What little commentary it has elicited has been confined to notes and incidental remarks—in short, to critical marginalia. Here is the text of Riddle 12:

> Fotum ic fere,　　foldan slite,
> grene wongas,　　þenden ic gæst bere.
> Gif me feorh losað,　　fæste binde
> swearte wealas,　　hwilum sellan men.
> Hwilum ic deorum　　drincan selle
> beorne of bosme,　　hwilum mec bryd triedeþ
> felawlonc fotum,　　hwilum feorran broht
> wonfeax wale　　wegeð ond þyð,
> dol druncmennen　　deorcum nihtum,
> wæteð in wætre,　　wyrmeð hwilum
> fægre to fyre;　　me on fæðme sticaþ
> hygegalan hond,　　hwyrfeð geneahhe,
> swifeþ me geond sweartne.　　Saga hwæt ic hatte,

þe ic lifgende   lond reafige
ond æfter deaðe   dryhtum þeowige.[29]

(I walk with feet, slit the earth, the green fields, while I bear a spirit. If life is loosed from me, I bind fast the dark *wealas,* sometimes better men. Sometimes I give a bold (also: dear, excellent) man to drink from my bosom; sometimes a woman treads me, very proud (also: stately, lustful) with her feet; sometimes a dark-haired *wale,* brought from afar, silly drunken slave, moves and presses (me) on dark nights, wets (me) in water, warms (me) at times, fairly by the fire; the lustful one's hand sticks in my embrace, turns often, moves through me, the dark one. Say what I am called, I who, living, plunder the land and, dead, serve people.)

Like many Old English riddles, this one is constituted by a complex series of conceptual oppositions. The first antithesis is articulated in lines 1–4: alive, the riddle subject "slits the earth, the green fields"; dead, it "binds fast the dark *wealas,* sometimes better men." In lines 5–13 we meet three figures whom the riddle subject serves in its "dead" life as a leather object of various kinds: the bold man whom it gives to drink from its bosom, the very proud woman who treads it with her feet, and finally, in the double-entendre section of the riddle, the dark-haired serving-woman who works the leather object on one level and masturbates on the other. In each case, the object in question is a leather receptacle of some kind which serves the bodies of its masters, becoming finally incorporated in the body of the *wonfeax wale.* While the implicitly well-to-do figures of the *deorum beorne* and *felawlonc bryd* are presented favorably, the *wealas* and the *wale* are singled out pejoratively. The dark-haired *wale* contrasts with the dark *wealas* of line 4, making one final opposition: the subject which "binds fast" male slaves is handled by a slave woman.

Let us now consider the double-entendre section. Numerous attempts have been made to identify the leather object described in lines 7b–13a: "glove," "jerkin," "hat," "boots," "bed-covering," even "coin purse."[30] On the other hand, the sexual identity of this object (female genitalia) and the sexual activity engaged in by the *wonfeax wale* (masturbation) have never, to my knowledge, been named. Williamson's comment is typical in this regard: "Though the riddle itself is not usually classified as 'obscene,' the double entendre of these lines should be clear."[31] While the academic must abide by the dictates of intellectual decorum, the translator need not. In his translation of the Exeter Book riddles, Williamson provides a rendering of the passage in question which more freely reveals its sexual dimension:

> Sometimes the dark-haired, drunken slave
> Lifts me up near the night fire
> With hot hands—turns, teases,
> Presses, thrusts, warm and wet,
> Down dark ways.[32]

Riddle 12 is a meditation of sorts on the subjects of slavery, sexuality, and the body—the physical enslavement of the *wealas* and the physical "liberation," through masturbation, of the *wonfeax wale*. And yet the term "meditation" does not do justice to a text which is so blatantly prejudiced. The conceptual opposition between the subject who binds slave men and yet is handled by a slave woman—is founded on another series of oppositions. The first term is culturally sanctioned, necessary, legally binding: dark male slaves, and "sometimes better men," are "bound fast." By contrast, the drunken dark-haired slave woman, masturbating by the fire, represents all that is culturally transgressive, supplementary, "unbound." Paralleling the movement from the *wealh* to the *wale* is the transformation of the riddle subject: from the virile ox which cuts the green fields and the hard leather which binds male slaves to the soft skin which serves the slave woman's pleasure.

Williamson's characterization of the riddle subject makes use of the oppositions nature/culture, source/supplement, and masculine/feminine: "The ox . . . seems to hold a savage and sensuous power. Alive, it ravages the land in an act of regenerative plunder. Dead, it offers its supple skin as a pleasure for man."[33] The ox moves from the living, the virile, the aggressive, and the productive, to the dead, the soft, the passive, and the pleasurable. One wonders, however, about Williamson's paraphrase, "dead, it offers its supple skin as a pleasure *for man*": in an effort to streamline the opposition between the masculine ox and the feminine leather, he misses, or rather overwrites, the transgressive moment of the text. Far from offering its supple skin as a pleasure "for man," the riddle subject serves the pleasure of a *woman*. Even more to the point is Williamson's comment that here the subject "thrusts against the lecherous slave-girl who comes to warm, wet, and work over her lord's new skin."[34] This paraphrase amounts to a wholesale rewriting of the text. The *wale* has been rendered a slave *girl*, the job of "thrusting" has been given to the riddle subject, a "lord" has been invented for the servant woman, and the sexual activity described in the riddle is transformed into what sounds very much like the *wale*'s service to her lord's penis. The text makes no mention of a lord who owns this "new skin," and that is precisely the point: the *wale* here is the riddle subject's master. She is, in fact, her own master; far from serving her lord, she serves herself.[35]

Having just criticized a series of gratuitous critical gestures I want to present some thoughts on the "gratuitous" rhetoric of the riddle itself. A good place to begin is with the phrase *dol druncmennen*. While *dol* is a well-attested word meaning "foolish" or "stupid," *druncmennen* is a *hapax legomenon*. Nonetheless, most scholars unquestioningly translate it as "drunken servingwoman."[36] Why have such a word? And why use it here? Why is the *wonfeax wale* singled out for such contempt? Why is she drunk? Why is she foolish or stupid? Because she is a servant? Because she is a woman? Because she masturbates? In a recent essay which argues that the Old English sexual riddles provide evidence of "wholesome and spontaneous" attitudes about female sexuality, Edith Whitehurst Williams asserts that the *wale* is represented as foolish and drunk not because she is a woman, but because she is a servant, implying that Riddle 12 is not misogynist, but classist.[37] I see no way in which such a distinction can be made. There are at least four possible reasons for the *wale*'s condemnation, all of which intersect, and none of which can be confidently excluded: her gender, her status as a servant, her ethnicity (if she is understood to be Welsh), and her sexual activity.

We can shed more light on the *wale*'s condemnation by comparing Riddle 12 with sexual riddles in which male servants are represented. The subject of Riddle 63, typically solved as "wine glass," speaks of being taken into a closet by a "good servant" (*tillic esne*) who proceeds to "work his will" with it. Although manuscript damage has rendered much of this riddle illegible, it seems to be based on an analogy between stealthy drinking and stealthy love-making:

> Oft ic secga   seledreame sceal
> fægre onþeon,   þonne ic eom forð boren
> glæd mid golde,   þær guman drincað
> Hwilum mec on cofan   cysseð muþe

tillic esne,   þær wit tu beoþ,
fæðme on folm. . . . . grum þyð,
wyrceð his willa. . . . . . ð l. . . . . .
. . . . fulre,   þonne ic forð cyme
. . . .
Ne mæg ic þy miþan, ...
. . . . an on leohte
. . . .
swylce eac bið sona   . . . .
. . r. te getacnad,   hwæt me to . . . .
. . . . leas rinc,   þa unc geryde wæs.

(Often I must fairly serve the hall-joy of men, when I am carried forth, shining (or: glad) with gold, where men drink. At times a good servant kisses me with his mouth in a closet where we two are, presses me (with fingers) in his hand's embrace, works his will . . . full, when I come forth . . . I can't conceal that, . . . in the light . . . likewise it will soon be (clearly) revealed, what the (?-) less man . . . to me, when it was pleasant for us.)[38]

The description of this servant as *tillic* is just as gratuitous as the description of the *wale* in Riddle 12 as *dol*, especially since his "work" produces only pleasure (*willan*), a pleasure which might be said to impede productivity. The two sections of the riddle form an interesting set of oppositions. In lines 1–3 the subject serves the public pleasure of men drinking in the hall—aristocratic men, if we are to go by the reference to the wine cup's gold demeanor (*glæd mid golde*). In the much longer second section of the riddle the subject serves the desire of the *tillic esne* in the private space of the *cofa* or closet. If we complete the fragmentary word. . . . *leas* in the last line, as Trautmann does, to read *receleas* (reckless), the "useful man-servant" appears as a transgressive figure.[39] On the non-sexual level, there would seem to be a violation of the taboo against drinking in private, or against drinking in a nobleman's house (although precisely because it is violated in private, this taboo is paradoxically also respected). There may also be a violation that involves class and sexuality: the male servant seeks illicit sexual gratification from the wine glass/aristocratic woman.[40] To sum up this comparison, both Riddle 12 and Riddle 63 feature transgressive subjects of the servant class who drink and engage in sexual activity, but whereas the *esne* of Riddle 63 is presented in a favorable light, the *wale* in Riddle 12 is ridiculed. This contradiction would seem to be squarely sex-based.

In Riddle 54, which has always belonged to the canonical set of double-entendre riddles, we find our *tillic esne* at work once again—this time with a butter churn: the churning of butter is represented as sexual intercourse:

> Hyse cwom gangan,   þær he hie wisse
> stondan in wincsele,   stop feorran to,
> hror hægstealdmon,   hof his agen
> hrægl hondum up,   hrand under gyrdels
> hyre stondendre   stiþes nathwæt,
> worhte his willan;   wagedan buta.
> Þegn onnette,   wæs þragum nyt
> tillic esne,   teorode hwæþre
> æt stunda gehwam   strong ær þon hio,
> werig þæs weorces.   Hyre weaxan ongon
> under gyrdelse   þæt oft gode men
> ferðþum freogað   ond mid feo bicgað.

(A young man came walking to where he knew her to be standing in the corner, the strong bachelor stepped forward from afar, lifted up his own garment, thrust something hard under her belt while she stood there; they both shook. The thane hastened, was at times useful, the good servant, but always, strong though he was, tired before her, weary of the work. Under her belt grew what good men often love with their hearts and buy with money.)

Tillic means not only "good" but "capable," that is, useful, productive. Here sexual activity is represented as useful work. This is not surprising since it is procreative: the man's churning helps to produce butter and a child. The offspring is then described as something which "good men often love with their hearts and buy with money." Riddle 54 represents procreation as a commercial activity governed by "good men." Here, then, we have a reason for the *wale*'s condemnation which involves precisely the intersection of class and gender: her sexual gratification does not involve men, it lies outside the circuit of production and procreation.

I want to conclude by considering, in light of Riddle 12, some comments recently offered by Elaine Tuttle Hansen on the subject of ideology in the Old English riddles. Hansen points out that "social conflicts" and "feared or problematic situations" provide the riddles with much of their subject matter. Through the use of prosopopoeia, such conflicts are displaced from the realm of the human to the non-human, "where they can be safely, even pleasurably, examined." She concludes:

> Despite this apparently playful treatment, then, many of the riddles im-
> plicitly and indirectly and collectively address a critical contradiction
> taken up in all wisdom literatures and perhaps heightened by the impor-
> tation of Christian ideology into a troubled social reality: the tension be-
> tween the affirmation and celebration of order and justice, on the one
> hand, and the experience of evil, suffering, and instability, on the
> other.[41]

The opposition Hansen erects between "order and justice" on the one hand and "evil, suffering, and instability" on the other is insufficient and misleading. Riddle 12 demonstrates that "evil, suffering, and in-stability" are sometimes the *predicates* of social order, insofar as this order requires the subjection and servitude of the *wealas*. Moreover, the crucial contradiction which this riddle stages is not between "order" and "suffering" but between "order" and "pleasure." Social order is perverted when the *wonfeax wale* assumes the power to satisfy her own desire, and reaffirmed through the repudiation of her pleasure. Hansen is certainly correct in pointing out that the prosopopoeic riddles often displace human conflict onto the non-human world, enabling this con-flict to be "safely, even pleasurably, examined." But in Riddle 12 it is not conflict, but *pleasure itself* that is displaced, and *within* the sphere of the human—from a literary community that was primarily Anglo-Saxon, male, and free, to the fictional, private realm of the (possibly Welsh), female, and enslaved *wale*.

Conclusion

The Exeter Book riddles have traditionally been read as a supple-ment to the canon of Old English literature. That is to say, critics have regarded them as capable of providing us with information that is con-cealed for various reasons where canonical texts are concerned. The riddles have been read as a repository of "native speech," as windows which reveal pleasing pictures of the Anglo-Saxon social landscape, and especially as a record of "frank" sexual representations not to be found elsewhere. Such readings attempt to recover what is marginal and suppressed in Old English literature and life, but also to naturalize this marginal and suppressed content. And the rhetoric of naturalization requires that we ignore, or treat as accidental, the fact that what is marginal has been marginalized in the first place. I have endeavored to show that, far from accurately representing the margins of Anglo-Saxon society, Riddle 12 makes their very marginality a prime feature of its rhetoric. The intersecting and mutually reinforcing margins of race, class, and gender all leave their traces in the *wonfeax wale* as a literary figure. This figure is the locus of an extraordinary and paradoxical fantasy: that of a subject so enslaved to the law that she is quite capable of toppling it.

Notes

1. *The Riddles of the Exeter Book,* ed. Frederick Tupper, Jr. (Boston: Ginn, 1910), lxxxvi.

2. Charles W. Kennedy, *An Anthology of Old English Poetry* (New York: Oxford University Press, 1960), 39.

3. Bruce Mitchell and Fred C. Robinson, *A Guide to Old English,* 4th rev. ed. (Oxford: Blackwell, 1986), 216.

4. Seth Lerer, *Literacy and Power in Anglo-Saxon Literature* (Lincoln: University of Nebraska Press, 1991), 101, 123. In the conclusion to this study, Lerer notes: "My book has also left out certain texts and contexts which, it might be argued, could provide the foil for literacy as I characterize it. As it stands, mine is a study of elite traditions: ones that privilege spiritual commitment, linguistic training, or runic skill" (198).

5. Lerer, 101.

6. Lerer, 101.

7. *The Riddles of the Exeter Book,* li.

8. *The Riddles of the Exeter Book,* 203. Note too the comment by Kevin Crossley-Holland in *The Exeter Book Riddles* (Harmondsworth, England: Penguin, 1979): "The implication of 'southerner' in line 6 has not been established; some critics think the word *superne* means simply a foreign man, or a servant; someone, anyhow, whose behaviour is un-English!" (126).

9. Ann Harleman Stewart, "Double Entendre in the Old English Riddles," *Lore and Language* 3 (1983): 48–49.

10. *The Riddles of the Exeter Book,* 95. The second sentence in this passage is quoted by Craig Williamson, *The Old English Riddles of the Exeter Book* (Chapel Hill: University of North Carolina Press, 1977), 167.

11. All quotations of the riddles are from George Philip Krapp and Elliott van Kirk Dobbie, ed., *The Exeter Book,* vol. 3 of *The Anglo-Saxon Poetic Records* (New York: Columbia University Press, 1936). All translations, unless otherwise noted, are my own.

12. "The Semantic Development of Old English *Wealh*," *Leeds Studies in English*, New Series 8 (1975): 30.

13. F. York Powell, contributor to *Social England*, ed. H. D. Traill, vol. 1 (New York: Putnam's, 1902), 125.

14. Agop Hacikyan, *A Linguistic and Literary Analysis of Old English Riddles* (Montreal: Casalini, 1966), 39.

15. Bogislav von Lindheim, "Traces of Colloquial Speech in Old English," *Anglia* 70 (1951): 23.

16. Von Lindheim was the first to argue that *wlanc* possessed the meaning "lustful, greedy" (in a sexual or non-sexual sense) as well as "proud, stately," citing three instances in the riddles where the sexual meaning alone is operative (Riddle 25, l. 7, Riddle 42, l. 4, and Riddle 45, l. 4). Elsewhere in the poetry he finds the sense "lustful" only in *Genesis A* 1825. See also Michael von Rüden, *Wlanc und Derivate im Alt- und Mittelenglischen: Eine wortgeschichtliche Studie* (Frankfurt: Lang, 1978), 143–46. Since *gal* and its derivatives came to denote the sin of lust, it is of course commonly found in homiletic texts. In the poetry this sense of *gal* is found in *Judith* 62, 256 and Riddle 12, l. 12. For instances in which *neb*, *þyrel*, and *wamb* are used in a sexual context see Riddles 44, 63, and 91.

17. von Lindheim, 26.

18. Craig Williamson, *A Feast of Creatures: Anglo-Saxon Riddle-Songs* (Philadelphia: University of Pennsylvania Press, 1982), 22.

19. *The Old English Riddles of the Exeter Book*, 299.

20. "De witzige Funktion des zweideutig-obszönen Rätsels besteht darin, daß der Rätsellöser praktisch immer als der Dumme dasteht. Kommt er nur auf die 'richtige', d.h. harmlose Lösung, wird er wegen seines schlichten Gemüts verlacht. Verfällt er, wie vom Rätselsteller beabsichtigt, auf die 'falsche', d.h. die unanständige, obszöne Lösung, verlacht man ihn wegen seiner schlichten Phantasie und hält ihm die 'richtige', d.h. die harmlose Lösung entgegen." Reinhard Gleissner, *Die "zweideutigen" altenglischen Rätsel des Exeter Book in ihrem zeitgenössischen Kontext* (Frankfurt: Lang, 1984), 14. (Translations of Gleissner are my own.)

21. "Es sind solche Rätsel zweideutig, die den Hörer ziemlich eindeutig auf eine erotische Lösung hinführen, um ihn dann mit der 'eigentlichen' anständigen Lösung erst recht bloßzustellen" (10).

22. Ann Harleman Stewart makes use of this model as well: "The sexual solution to one of these riddles is not the 'real' solution; thus, when the decipherer arrives at an obscene solution, the riddler can disclaim all responsibility for it. Ha! he can say, in effect, it's all in your mind: the real solution is *this*— and produce an innocent referent like an onion, a key, or a churn" ("Double Entendre," 49).

23. "Die Funktion des zweideutig-obszönen Rätsels als Witz erlaubt auch, mit ihm gegen den Stachel der als lästig empfundenen Norm eines sexuellen Tabus zu löcken. Hier wird das Tabu und die hinter dem Tabu stehende Norm durch den Witz angegriffen und verletzt, wobei das durch den Witz hervorgerufene Lachen befreiend wirkt. Jedoch geht die durch den Witz verursachte Normabweichung nie so weit, daß die Norm selbst letztlich abgeschafft werden soll. Der Witz braucht, um als solcher verstanden werden und funktionieren zu

können, die Norm, von der er sich absetzt und gegen die er angeht. Auf der anderen Seite muß zur gesetzten Norm bereits eine gewisse Distanz bestehen, die es erlaubt, sie zu verspotten'' (14).

24. The concept of the projection of lack onto woman stems, of course, not from Freud or Lacan, but from the feminist psychoanalytic criticism of scholars such as Jane Gallop and Kaja Silverman. Freud's theory of sexual jokes is both sexist and classist. As so often, his work is useful as an analysis not of the truth of patriarchy, but of its artifice. See Sigmund Freud, "Jokes and Their Relation to the Unconscious," *Standard Edition of the Complete Psychological Works of Sigmund Freud*, ed. James Strachey and trans. James Strachey et al. (London: Hogarth, 1953–74), vol. 8 of 24.

25. For bibliography on Riddle 20, see the notes in Williamson's edition (193–99) as well as Marie Nelson, "Old English Riddle 18 (20): A Description of Ambivalence" *Neophilologus* 66 (1982): 291–300. Riddle 42 has been most recently interpreted by Lerer in *Literacy and Power*, 115–25. Gleissner has offered a reading of Riddle 46 in *Die zweideutigen altenglischen Rätsel*, 299–337. A cursory reading of Riddle 63 is provided by Stewart, "Double Entendre," 45–46. Riddle 91 is discussed by Edith Whitehurst Williams, "What's So New about the Sexual Revolution?" in *New Readings on Women in Old English Literature*, ed. Helen Damico and Alexandra Hennessey Olsen (Bloomington: Indiana University Press, 1990), 141–44. Riddle 77 has not, to my knowledge, ever been treated as a sexual riddle, although Gregory K. Jember lists one of its solutions as "female genitalia" in the appendix to *The Old English Riddles: A New Translation* (Denver: Society for New Language Study, 1976).

26. *The Old English Riddles of the Exeter Book*, 210.

27. Stewart, 42.

28. *A Feast of Creatures*, 178.

29. My text of Riddle 12 differs from the *ASPR* edition in one important respect. Although the words *wealh* and *wale* can mean "Welsh person" as well as "servant," obviously the one sense does not necessarily include the other. This raises the question of whether or not to capitalize the word. In order to preserve the ambiguity I have chosen to use the uncapitalized form.

30. "Glove" is proposed by Tupper (96) and Gleissner (341), "jerkin" and "hat" by August Prehn, "Komposition und Quellen der Rätsel des Exeterbuches," *Neuphilologische Studien* 3 (1883): 176–77, "boots" by A. J. Wyatt, ed., *Old English Riddles* (Boston, 1912), 73; "bed-covering" by Christine Fell, *Women in Anglo-Saxon England* (Bloomington: Indiana University Press, 1984), 67; and "coin purse" by Moritz Trautmann, ed., *Die Altenglischen Rätsel (die Rätsel des Exeterbuches)* (Heidelberg, 1915), 75.

31. *The Old English Riddles of the Exeter Book*, 167. Gleissner and Tupper make similar comments. Von Lindheim remarks that after line 7 the riddle becomes "leeringly obscene, even if the second solution intended by the author remains vague" (34). However, in a brief review of sexual imagery in the riddles, Stewart observes that Riddles 12 and 63 mention "that part of (a woman's anatomy) referred to as *fæðm*" (47).

32. *A Feast of Creatures*, 70. As this rendering suggests, one might argue that the *wale* masturbates *with* the leather object in question (as opposed to

42   *John W. Tanke*

reading it as a figure for her genitalia). Such is the implication of Kevin Crossley-Holland's translation: "sometimes a slave-girl, raven-haired, brought far from Wales, cradles and presses me—some stupid, sozzled maid-servant, she fills me with water on dark nights, warms me by the gleaming fire; on my breast she places a wanton hand and writhes about, then sweeps me against her dark declivity" (34).

33. *A Feast of Creatures*, 170.

34. *A Feast of Creatures*, 170.

35. Certain linguistic details may be adduced in support of my reading of the *wale* as a transgressive figure. The phrase *wegeð ond þyð* (moves and presses) also occurs in Riddle 19, whose subject is, interestingly enough, the plough: it speaks of being moved and pressed by its master, the ploughman. Moreover the word *þyð* also occurs in two other sexual riddles (61 and 62) where it indicates masculine sexual activity. There is also the curious word *sweartne* in line 13, which the majority of editors read as governed by the preceding *me*. If this reading is correct, the riddle subject is represented as masculine!

36. Trautmann notes that this interpretation stems from C. W. M. Grein's *Sprachschatz*. His suggestion that the word might mean "*die Schenkin*" (with allowance for the existence in OE of **drunc* alongside *drinc*) has not been responded to. See Moritz Trautmann, ed., *Die altenglischen Rätsel (Die Rätsel des Exeterbuches)* (Heidelberg, 1915), 75.

37. "What's So New about the Sexual Revolution?" 141. Williams reasons that the *wale* is condemned solely on the basis of class since the word *gal* (lascivious) is nowhere used of upper-class women in the other double-entendre riddles. This rationale assumes that class and gender do not intersect to begin with, that misogyny cannot hide behind classism. Williams does not comment on the nature of the sexual activity represented in Riddle 12.

38. Parts of this riddle are unrecoverable, but all editors agree on the restoration of two partially recorded words (indicated in parentheses in my translation): *fingrum* (with fingers) for MS . . . *grum* in line 6, and *torhte* (clearly) for MS ..*r* . *te* in line 14. For a review of attempts to restore other passages, see Krapp and Dobbie's edition, 367.

39. Krapp and Dobbie note: "The evidence of the MS. makes (*rece)leas* very probable in l. 15a" (367).

40. There is some evidence to suggest that the wine glass is personified as a feminine subject. On the one hand, the role of women as dispensers of wine and beer in the royal hall is a well-established topos in Old English poetry generally; on the other, the fragmentary word *-fulre* may be a feminine form, governed by the gender of the speaking wine glass. If this is the case, however, the use of *glæd* in line 3 is a problem, since a woman (real or imaginary) would have to say: *gladu*. Suffice to say that the Exeter Book riddles consistently problematize the relation of grammatical to "natural" gender. For more on this quite interesting, but vexed, topic see Moritz Trautmann, "Das Geschlecht in den Altenglischen Rätseln," *Beiblatt zur Anglia* 25 (1914): 324–27, and Tupper's comments in *The Riddles of the Exeter Book,* lxxxix-xc.

41. *The Solomon Complex: Reading Wisdom in Old English Poetry* (Toronto: University of Toronto Press, 1988), 137.

Exile and the Semiosis of Gender in Old English Elegies

* * *

Helen T. Bennett

The gendered nature of exile as presented in four Old English elegies—
The Wanderer, The Seafarer, The Wife's Lament, and *Wulf and Eadwacer*—points to the gendered nature of class in Anglo-Saxon society.
Moreover, in light of contemporary semiotic and literary theory, scholarly investigations of these issues by members of the academic community themselves create intersections with class and gender issues
operating in the present.

Wills, law codes, and historical chronicles from the Anglo-Saxon period, while predictably focusing more on the rights and activities of
male members of society, do tell us something about Anglo-Saxon
women, at least those from the aristocratic class. These women exer-
cised considerable power, relatively speaking, in both secular and religious spheres.[1] Yet, the heroic society that forms the backdrop for *The
Wander* and *The Seafarer* is dominated by one class—the warrior
class—and one relationship—between lord and thane. A society based
on an economy of war is a society of men, a society in which masculinity itself becomes the only class. In this society, being a woman
means being an exile, since there is no role for woman in a society predicated on war and death. By celebrating the warrior society, then, poetry excludes women from the social picture more thoroughly than did
actual history, insofar as we can retrieve or interpret historical reality.

This suppression of the female presence has been perpetuated, and
indeed enhanced, by a scholarly tradition that has dominated until very
recently.[2] Just as there was no place for a woman in the Anglo-Saxon
warrior society of literature, there was no place for a woman scholar
who wanted to read as a woman. To gain legitimacy and prestige, the
female scholar, like the medieval nun or abbess, had to deny her gender
by following prescribed patriarchal research methods to complete pre-

scribed patriarchal research projects. Today there are still gender asymmetries within the class of academic professionals, in terms of promotions and salaries, and in terms of critical perspective: we speak of feminist criticism but have no widely accepted equivalent to name the inescapable genderedness of the masculine perspective. Feminist criticism has, however, served to highlight gender as essential to the semiotic process of any critical interpretation,[3] and has thus redefined the parameters of any scholarly consensus that will be reached in the future.

In this chapter, I will explore the gendered nature of semiosis in both sign creation and sign reception as represented in the four elegies. I will analyze exile as a gloss on the gender asymmetries within Anglo-Saxon social (class) and semiotic structures. We will see that the male exiles, even while on the margins of society, participate in the social and linguistic codes that give form and create meaning; the female exiles constitute a challenge to social and linguistic structure. First, the men have a clearer social role against which to define their exile, just as their exile has its own rules that in turn help define society (they, in fact, come to constitute a sub-class of warrior within society); second, the men's exiled status, unlike the women's exclusion, is resolved by membership in a new (Christian) community; and, third, the men express their situation in a language better able to articulate their experience than the women's. Lastly, invoking the psychoanalytic and semiotic theories of Julia Kristeva, Jacques Lacan, Roman Jakobson, and Charles S. Peirce, I will relate the class and gender issues raised by the elegies to our own social and interpretive world.

Anglo-Saxon society is organized for war. It depends, in fact, on war for the very survival of its structure.[4] Tribes and kingdoms constantly engage in feuds; thanes aspire to fight well, and, when necessary, to die with and for their lord (as stated, for example, in *The Battle of Maldon*). When they fight loyally, they are supported and rewarded by their lord/king. Within the legal and social structure of Anglo-Saxon warrior society, the man without a lord seems to be virtually without an identity; he no longer signifies. Both *The Seafarer* and *The Wanderer* define their semiotic limbo by motion—as instability: they are wave-tossed as opposed to being on the solid base of social community. Although the speaker of *The Wanderer* more explicitly expresses longing for the lost stability and security of the lord-thane relationship,[5] both he and the seafarer contrast their current cold and isolation with the warmth and community of the mead-hall shared with kinsmen and their treasure-giving lord (*Wand.* 8a–38b; *Seaf.* 12b–30b). Yet, even the most tender memories of the wanderer indicate the formal, ritual, coded nature of the relationships between lord and thane. The wanderer remembers

> þæt he his mondryhten
> clyppe ond cysse,   ond on cneo lecge
> honda ond heafod,   swa he hwilum ær
> in geardagum   giefstolas breac.
> (41b–44)

> that he embraced and
> kissed his liege lord, and on his knee
> lay (his) hands and head, as he formerly,
> in bygone days, enjoyed the gift-stool (throne).

Furthermore, the conventional gestures enacted here mark a society whose class structure is defined by one's relationship to death.

A society based on tribal warfare inevitably produces exiles, so the coded role of the male does not actually end with his exile. The very possibility of a warrior's exclusion from society helps define that society's structure. Robert Bjork suggests that exile caused by the conventional occurrence of feud is itself a "constant tradition in the Anglo-Saxon world," "an accepted (even expected) part of Anglo-Saxon life," and "ties [the wanderer] to the social order" through "rigid rules of exile" which govern his ideas and behavior. These rules, attested by other Old English poems which Bjork cites, include the exile's suffering pain and maintaining silence (119–21).[6] Thus, the male exile still occupies a slot within the class structure and semiotic code of his society.

Women in this warrior society have the non-roles of (failed) peaceweaver and mourner for the dead produced by feud. They become part of the treasure dispensed by the victorious ruler, or are otherwise utilized within the warrior economy.[7] So, unlike the men, the female exiles in *The Wife's Lament* and *Wulf and Eadwacer* present no clearcut contrast between a past inclusion in society and a present exile, between past joy and present sorrow. Instead, the speakers portray a history of ambivalent relations with their societies and their mates, expressed in personal, emotional terms, transcending social ritual.

The women are stationary, not storm-tossed, but lack of movement here does not reflect stability: they are being forced to stay in a place against their will. In *Wulf and Eadwacer* the speaker is currently sep-

arated from her lover (?) Wulf (4), and she speaks of a history of
mourning his absence (14); she recalls a past embrace by a man (who
may or may not be Wulf) with a mixture of joy and loathing; in terms
of the future, she fears hostility between her people and Wulf, if he tries
to come to her; and she fears Wulf's causing her separation from her
hwelp (16). The wife in *The Wife's Lament* tells of her lord leaving her
(6–8), his people trying to cause enmity between herself and her lord
(11–14), and her own lord ordering her into a friendless exile (15–17a).
Both women's relationships to their societies are further problematized
by the possibility that their marriages are exogamous, a theory encouraged by the references to "my people" (*Leodum . . . minum W&E* 1)
and "his people" (*þæs monnes magas WL* 11).[8]

The conclusions of the four elegies further develop the contrasting
relations of men and women to their cultural codes and class structures.
In *The Wanderer* and *The Seafarer,* we see a smooth transition from the
patriarchal Germanic warrior society to the Christian society, as exile
becomes the metaphor for the general human condition of seeking God.
The dissolution of earthly structure and meaning leads to the acknowl-
edgment that security in this world is transitory and that lasting security must instead be sought in eternal community with God. *The
Wanderer* ends with the gnomic advice

> Wel bið þam þe him are seceð,
> frofre to fæder on heofonum,   þær us eal seo
> fæstnung stondeð.
> (114b–15)

Well is it for him who seeks mercy, comfort from Father in heaven,
where for us all security (fastness) stands.

The voice in *The Seafarer* urges

> Uton we hycgan   hwær we ham agen,
> ond þonne geþencan   hu we þider cumen,
> ond we þonne eac tilien,   þæt we to moten
> in þa ecan   eadignesse,
> þær is lif gelong   in lufan dryhtnes,
> hyht in heofonum.
> (117–22a)

Let us think where we have our home,
and then think how we may come there,

and then strive that we may [come] to
eternal happiness, where life derives
from the love of God, joy in heaven.

Both poems present a new and enduring idealized society, seemingly
without class or gender, whose members, including even the reader or
audience through the use of *we* (us), all stand as equal thanes before the
lord God, who will never be killed off in a feud. However, the *all*-
inclusive *we* in fact privileges men: although the wanderer speaks of all
human life—male and female—as fleeting (109), the poem's portrait
of the universal exile is based on a class whose membership is restricted
to men (the thane/warrior class); and, in *The Seafarer,* women are mentioned as part of the package deal that constitutes the transitory, earthly
joy lost to the exile when the seafarer sets out to sea:

> Ne biþ him to hearpan hyge   ne to hringþege,
> ne to wife wyn   ne to worulde hyht,
> ne ymbe owiht elles,   nefne ymb ỹða gewealc,
> ac a hafað longunge   se þe on lagu fundað.
> (*Seaf.* 44–47)

> His thoughts are not of the harp, nor of
> the receiving of rings, nor of delight in woman,
> nor of joy in the world, nor of anything else,
> except of the rolling of the waves, but he always
> has longing who sets out on the ocean.

Thus, *The Wanderer* and *The Seafarer* recreate in heaven the exclusively male class system of earthly society.

Neither *The Wife's Lament* nor *Wulf and Eadwacer* contains any references to God or heaven; no end to exile or insecurity is sought from
above, in keeping with the formulation of woman within the larger
Judeo-Christian tradition.[9] Julia Kristeva argues that the Judeo-
Christian triumph marked the repression of maternal deities and the
erection of a patriarchal monotheism which depends on the definition
of *woman* as all that is disorderly, all that transgresses limits and threatens symbolic order:

> without this gap between the sexes, without this localization of the poly-
> morphic, orgasmic body, desiring and laughing, in the *other* sex, it
> would have been impossible, in the *symbolic realm*, to isolate the prin-

ciple of One Law—the One, Sublimating, Transcendent Guarantor of
the ideal interests of the community.[10]

Because of her physical, corporal, and sexual nature, woman, according to Kristeva, has always been cut off from the law and codes gov-
erning social groupings more symbolic than the immediate, bodily
union of man and woman or woman and child, i.e., codes of class
structure.[11] Thus, in a way, Kristeva is saying that woman has always
constituted a class outside the class system, that gender has always
been class. Furthermore, Kristeva connects woman's exclusion from
social class to her exclusion from the class system in heaven. Woman

> has no direct relation with the law of the community and its political and
> religious unity: God generally speaks only to men. Which is not to say
> that woman doesn't know more about Him; indeed, she is the one who
> knows the material conditions, as it were, of the body, sex, and procre-
> ation, which permit the existence of the community, its permanence and
> thus man's very dialogue with God. . . . But woman's knowledge is cor-
> poral, aspiring to pleasure rather than tribal unity. . . . It is an unfor-
> mulable knowledge.[12]

This knowledge of God is not related to the *fæstnung* offered to the
wanderer or the seafarer. Just as the female Anglo-Saxon exiles could
not gain security from the earthly conventional lord/thane relationship,
so they cannot benefit from divine solace for the general human condition; the abstract, symbolic, patriarchal Word would not comfort
their "polymorphic, orgasmic body."[13]

In *Powers of Horror: An Essay on Abjection*,[14] Kristeva argues that
culture declares abject (horrifying, defiling) whatever "disturbs identity, system, order" (4). The exile is "the one by whom the abject exists" (8). The abject "shatters the wall of repression and its judgments";
it "is perverse because it neither gives up nor assumes a prohibition, a
rule, a law; but turns them aside, misleads, corrupts, uses them, takes
advantage of them, the better to deny them" (15). Within the Judeo-
Christian tradition, the abject includes bodily excretions that violate the
clear boundaries of the body; primary among them is menstrual blood.
Thus, by both their physical being and the absence of reconciliation to
the social structure at the end of their utterances, the wife and the
speaker in *W&E* fit Kristeva's description of the abject—the exile—in
ways that the male exiles do not.

Kristeva further links woman's exclusion from social class and religious (symbolic) structures to her exclusion from the language of grammar, linear syntax, conscious rules. For Kristeva and Jacques Lacan, these attributes offer only a partial and inadequate formulation of language which disregards the unconscious drives and biophysical processes. Lacan, who sees all humans as born into symbolic language through an alienation or exile from the mother,[15] sees woman as the greater exile because *woman* cannot be formulated in words: "There is no such thing as *The* woman, where the definite article stands for the universal. . . . There is woman only as excluded by the nature of things which is the nature of words."[16] The symbolic order, which includes words and things, is the province of man, who orders his world by his law. Using Lévi-Strauss, Lacan argues that, within this order, woman, as a commodity of exchange, is a signified without a signifier, analogous to a 'zero-symbol'.[17]

To challenge a patriarchal language that cannot signify woman, Kristeva advocates a language close to the body, which undermines structure by blurring boundaries, exploding codes, and promoting polysemy.[18] This apparent violation of structural principles, this refusal to clarify paradoxes, this insistence on presenting without resolving, differs from traditional language in a way strikingly similar to Roman Jakobson's description of *metonymy*, in contrast to *metaphor*, and both sets of contrasts illuminate the differences in the language of the four Old English elegies.

As defined by Jakobson, metaphor is based on similarity, and metonymy is based on contiguity. Similarity and contiguity, in fact, determine all linguistic signs. In an utterance we choose among *similar* signs and combine signs to form phrases and sentences: the constituents of the utterance are present in a contiguous context, those constituents having been selected from a set of similar (substitution) signs, which are present in the code but absent in the utterance itself.[19] Metonymic connections thus come from closeness; metaphoric connections come from coded similarities. Gillian Overing uses Jakobson to elaborate on the implications of this contrast. The metonymic mode is characterized by

> flexibility of association and meaning; resistance to conclusion or decisive interpretation; avoidance of interpreting one thing in terms of another in favor of seeing those things for themselves; deferral, which can

be indefinite, of resolving meaning into a static or fixed core; emphasis
on the here-and-now of immediate perception, on the process and experience of meaning construction rather than on its end-product. (8)

The metaphoric mode constitutes

the movement toward resolution of a juxtaposed dyad into a third over-
arching, meaning-encompassing element, the location of the experience
of interpretation in analysis, in the deferred gratification of achieved
meaning, an emphasis on product over process. (8)

Thus, the metonymic mode resembles the corporal, immediate, fluid
experience Kristeva sees as informing women's language, experience
in the "here-and-now," experience in process that defers arriving at a
conclusion; in contrast, the metaphoric mode moves toward resolution
and defers experience until the point at which a (final) meaning has
been achieved.

This difference between the metaphoric and metonymic modes is
manifested in the attitudes toward language implicit in the elegies, in
their treatment of the theme of union and separation, and in their conception of time.[20] Following the rules of exile, the wanderer repeatedly
mentions the importance of controlled speech.[21] A man must not be
overhasty in speech (*hrædwyrde* 66b); he must not boast until he clearly
knows which way the thought of his heart will turn (70–72). This restriction of language to the conscious and deliberate (and deferred) is
echoed by the voice offering Christian comfort at the end:

> ne sceal næfre his torn to rycene
> beorn of his breostum acyþan   nemþe he ær þa bote
>   cunne,
> eorl mid elne gefremman.
>   (112b–14a)

> a man shall never make known too quickly the resentment
> (sorrow) in his breast unless he, the earl, knows
> before how to perform the remedy vigorously (with
> courage).

The wanderer, therefore, must not speak until speech indicates that a
resolution has been determined. But the female speakers, perhaps because their speech cannot be bound by the laws of a patriarchal lan-

guage foreign to their existence, do speak freely, expressing the felt experience and not necessarily seeking closure.[22]

Thematically, *The Wanderer* and *The Seafarer* move "toward resolution of a juxtaposed dyad," by drawing equivalences between communities and states of exile, and by replacing elements from one realm of experience with those from another. The wanderer says, *Waraδ hine wræclast, nales wunden gold* (*Wand* 32) 'the path of exile possesses him, not at all the wound gold'; the seafarer says:

> Hwilum ylfete song
> dyde ic me to gomene,   ganetes hleoþor
> ond huilpan sweg   fore hleahtor wera,
> mæw singende   fore medodrince.
>
> (19b–22)

Sometimes the song of the swan gave me joy,
the sound of the gannet, and the music of the
curlew, instead of the laughter of men, the
sea-gull singing in place of meaddrink.

Hardships are *substituted* for the pleasures of the past. Yet the final metaphoric substitution is unity with God, who reconciles all differences, and who provides a divine equivalent to the earthly class system.

The Wife's Lament and *Wulf and Eadwacer* are all about longing for contiguity here and now in a world of separations. The wife endured the departure of her lord; she departed to seek protection; her man's kinsmen sought to separate her from her lord through enmity; this causes her longing. Her lord ordered her to stay in one place (separate from him). Their vows that nothing but death would separate them are broken (as if they never were). She endures hardships *feor ge neah* 'far and near' (25b). Thoughts of her lord's departure seize her with longing, as she envisions other couples together (32b–34). And, following her "gnomic" passage, she describes her man's solitary state.

In *Wulf and Eadwacer,* some *he* will be in danger if he comes (to the speaker); she laments that Wulf is on one island, while she is on another. She sits in one place as her 'widewandering thoughts' *widlastum wenum* (9) of Wulf torment her. Her being embraced (or laid about with branches) by the man whose identity is not clear causes conflicting emotions in the speaker; she is sickened by Wulf's absence (*seldcymas* 'seldom comings' [14b]). At the end, she worries about Wulf taking away the *earne hwelp* (16) to the woods.

Both poems end with the unresolved longing born of separation. In
fact, the separation has nullified any past union. The speaker in *Wulf
and Eadwacer* declares

> þæt mon eaþe tosliteð   þætte næfre gesomnad wæs,
> uncer giedd geador.
> (18–19a)
>
> (That) one may easily rend what never was joined,
> our song together.

Likewise, the wife says

> is nu * * *   swa hit no wære
> freondscipe uncer.
> (*WL* 24–25a)
>
> [it] is now   as if it never was
> our friendship.

And the *The Wife's Lament* ends with the image of separation and its
attendant sorrow:

> of langoþe   Wa bið þam þe sceal
>   leofes abidan.
> (52b–53)
>
> Woe be to him who must wait with longing
> for the beloved.

Resolution—or its lack—is linked to the treatment of time in the
four poems. Timelessness in God is offered as a salvation from this un-
reliable, changing world in the men's elegies, but the boundaries between time and timelessness (as well as between danger and security)
are blurred in the women's poems. Woven in among discrete events is
the collapse of linear time, in what Kristeva calls women's time, which
is cyclical and non-linear. *The Wife's Lament* defies attempts to recon-
struct the chronology of events,[23] in spite of the temporal markers (*ær-
est* [6], *þa* [9, 18], *nu* [4, 24], *þonne* [35]) and verb forms that reflect
a time sequence (*ongunnon* [11], *het* [15]). The wife will tell of hardships *niwes oþþe ealdes*; she has always suffered (*a* 5); she can never

rest (*ne æfre* 39); ever shall the young man suffer (*a* 42); *ful oft* (21, 32) implies recurrence, cycles, timelessness, as do the mirror images of the wife's exile and the young man's, the repetition of *bliþe gebæro* (21, 44), and the image of waiting indefinitely at the end. The last word of the poem is *abidan*.

Wulf and Eadwacer, like *The Wife's Lament,* contains just enough temporal markers to tease us into attempting a narrative reconstruction: a present of separation, a past of mourning for the absent beloved, a possible future of separation from the *hwelp*. But there is also disjunctive, cyclical, and eternal time—the conditional tense which takes place outside time (2, 7); the disjointed dramatic present of addressing two different listeners (13–15, 16–17 or 19); the refrain, which seems to create an interlace or cyclical structure; and the closing line—an atemporal generalization about separation and union.

The Wife's Lament and *Wulf and Eadwacer* have consistently been read, by both traditional and feminist critics, as the utterances of women,[24] despite the general assumption that all Anglo-Saxon *scops* were male, because the differences in the language used by the male and female elegiasts conform to the culture/nature, reason/emotion split common to the construction of gender in Western culture. However, the assumption of male authorship, along with assumptions about the social context of the utterances and value judgments on the language used, have been increasingly challenged by feminist critics and scholars.[25] These studies have demonstrated that the exclusively male class structure of Anglo-Saxon heroic society—including lord, thane, and *scop*—is partially a product of the modern academic tradition of literary interpretation.

The composition of the modern audience for Old English literature has thus brought to light the gendered nature of sign interpretation. But this revelation does not necessarily lead to a relativistic impasse in the search for meaning. The semiotic theories of Charles S. Peirce focus on sign interpretation as a triadic process, involving not only the signifier and the signified but the *interpretant,* the hypothesis or image that moves toward meaning. A final interpretant (meaning) will be determined at some future point by what Peirce calls the interpreting community, which consists of all qualified experts in the field.[26] Meanwhile, various interpretants swim along in a semiotic continuum. Individual members of the interpreting community necessarily have partial perspectives, but consensus, in the long run, protects against the

"vagaries of you and me".[27] Moreover, the community is itself evolv-
ing all the time, since "social mobility" is possible; theoretically, inclusion in this class is based not on gender or economic status, but on
expertise. As women become more and more numerous within the interpreting community, their perspectives gain increased representation
in the consensus called "meaning."

This version of semiosis is inclusive in a revolutionary way. Peirce
includes in semiosis both emotion and reason, process and product—
concepts associated with both genders. Ironically, Peirce's theories
themselves are subject to gendered readings. Jakobson uses Peirce, in
relation to metonymy and metaphor, to argue for two sets of interpretants for each sign: "There are two references which serve to interpret
the sign—one to the code and the other to the context, *whether coded
or free*" ("Two Aspects of Language," 99). This dichotomy parallels
the gender contrast I have been developing in terms of *code* (metaphor,
similarity, closure, maleness) and *context* (metonymy, contiguity, polysemy ["whether coded or free"], femaleness).

Overing sees Peirce as facilitating a non-hierarchical reconciliation
of the metonymic and metaphoric modes by including the reader in the
continual process of semiosis. One moves toward meaning, but recur-
sively and self-consciously (metonymically), and without ever actually
getting there (*Language, Sign, and Gender*, 57–60).

On the other hand, Michael Shapiro defines the concept of *markedness* as a species of Peirce's interpretant.[28] In any binary opposition,
so the argument goes, there is a perceived hierarchy or asymmetry:
one term in the opposition is more general, and therefore higher
(unmarked); the other is more specific, limited, and therefore lower
(marked).

The non-hierarchical reading of Peirce is by a woman, the hierarchical reading by a man. Perhaps equally significant is the example of
markedness—*man* versus *woman*—cited by Shapiro and others as if it
is an almost accidental choice among many other such possibilities.
Shapiro says, "This broader scope of the unmarked member is similarly reflected in lexical oppositions such as English *man* vs. *woman*,
where the former is the generic (unmarked) designation of humankind,
while the latter is reserved for the designation of only a subset of the
referential field" (16). Within this mindset, *woman* as marked is still
something of a social and semiotic outcast—or exile. But sign interpreters, unless otherwise conditioned, see themselves as unmarked;
markedness is itself determined by the sign-interpreting community,

and as that community evolves, so will the designation of markedness. Thus, in approaching the final interpretant of the Anglo-Saxon texts, we will be participating in a recursive process which will also help us better understand ourselves.

Notes

1. For an overview of recent historical work on Anglo-Saxon women, see my article "From Peace Weaver to Text Weaver: Feminist Approaches to Old English Studies," *Twenty Years of the "Year's Work in Old English Studies,"* ed. Katherine O'Brien O'Keeffe, *Old English Newsletter,* Subsidia 15 (1989): 23–42.

2. In *Desire for Origins* (New Brunswick: Rutgers University Press, 1990), Allen Frantzen describes how the patriarchal scholarly tradition applied Tacitus's geographically and chronologically distant description of Germanic society—as based on the *comitatus* relationship—to the world of *Beowulf* (174–76) as a way of creating the desired origins for Anglo-Saxon society. Clare A. Lees analyzes J. R. R. Tolkien's key role in the masculinization of *Beowulf* scholarship: in arguing for the artistic integrity of *Beowulf*, whose structure depends on the hero's battles with the monsters, Tolkien entirely omits the central episode concerning Grendel's mother. Tolkien thus erroneously creates an exclusively male Anglo-Saxon world for a presumably all-male audience, then and now. ("Men and *Beowulf*," in *Medieval Masculinities: Regarding Men in the Middle Ages,* ed. C. Lees [forthcoming]. My thanks to Professor Lees for allowing me access to this essay prior to its publication.)

3. See, for example, *Gender and Reading: Essays on Readers, Texts, and Contexts,* ed. Elizabeth A. Flynn and Patrocinio P. Schweikart (Baltimore: Johns Hopkins University Press, 1986). In relation to Anglo-Saxon studies, see my *OEN* article cited in note 1, and Helen T. Bennett, Clare A. Lees, and Gillian R. Overing, "Gender and Power: Feminism and Old English Studies," *Medieval Feminist Newsletter* (Fall 1990): 15–23.

In "Men and *Beowulf*," Lees demonstrates the continued importance of gender in reading and interpretation by contrasting two contemporary studies of *Beowulf:* James W. Earl, "*Beowulf* and the Origins of Civilization," *Speaking Two Languages: Traditional Disciplines and Contemporary Theory in Medieval Studies,* ed. Allen J. Frantzen (Albany: SUNY Press, 1991), 65–69; Gillian R. Overing's *Language, Sign and Gender in* Beowulf (Carbondale: Southern Illinois University Press, 1990).

4. "[W]arriors may produce death but their desires are channeled into a social ethos that ritualizes desire as heroic choice. . . . Warriors therefore choose death as a means of reproduction for the warrior caste" (Lees, "Men and *Beowulf*").

5. The seafarer expresses ambivalence about his situation:

> Forþon cnyssað nu
> heortan geþohtas,   þæt ic hean streamas,
> sealtyþa gelac   sylf cunnige;
> monað modes lust   mæla gehwylce
> ferð to feran,   þæt ic feor heonan
> elþeodigra   eard gesece.
>
> (33b–38)

> Therefore the thoughts
> of my heart beat, that I the high streams,
> the tumult of salt waves, myself seek;
> the desire of my mind urges   (at) every occasion
> to travel forth, that I far hence
> seek the land of foreigners.

All quotations from the Old English are from George Philip Krapp and Elliott Van Kirk Dobbie, eds., *The Anglo-Saxon Poetic Records* (New York: Columbia University Press, 1969). Translations are mine.

6. "*Sundor Æt Rune:* The Voluntary Exile of the Wanderer," *Neophilologus* 73 (1989): 119–21. Bjork also demonstrates that the sense of fulfillment from the lord-thane relationship extends to male scholars. He says, "Feud, of course, is a conventional, inevitable aspect of this society. And just as feuds are inevitable (*and thus desirable within the culture because of their validating power*), so is the grief resulting from them" (121). [Italics are mine.] Contrast Bjork to Lees's assessment quoted in note 4 above.

7. As Overing says, "Peace-weavers are assigned the role of creating peace, in fact, embodying peace, in a culture where war and death are privileged values" (84). Here Overing indicates that women are signifiers without a signified, referring to the "utter nonsignification of the women as peace-weaver": "[their] meaning as peace-weaver is *untranslatable*" (85). At best, then, woman as peace-weaver stands for a diminished cultural value, one that has little chance of being translated into reality. For the tradition of women as mourners, see my article "The Female Mourner at Beowulf's Funeral: Filling in the Blanks/Hearing the Spaces," *Exemplaria* 4.1 (March 1992): 35–50.

8. On the prevalence of exogamous marriages in Anglo-Saxon society, see Lorraine Lancaster, "Kinship in Anglo-Saxon Society," *British Journal of Sociology* 9 (1958): 230–50, esp. 241ff.

9. The suppression of the female perspective in the Judeo-Christian tradition is often discussed by feminist writers. See, for example, Carol P. Christ, "Symbols of Goddess and God in Feminist Theology," in *The Book of the Goddess Past and Present* (New York: Crossroad, 1989), 231–51; see also Carolyn Walker Bynum, "Introduction: The Complexity of Symbols," in *Gender and Religion: On the Complexity of Symbols,* ed. Carolyn Walker Bynum et al. (Boston: Beacon, 1986), 1–20.

10. Julia Kristeva, "About Chinese Women," *The Kristeva Reader,* ed. Toril Moi (New York: Columbia University Press, 1986), 141.

11. While women in Anglo-Saxon England enjoyed some legal rights, including the right to own property, there is no evidence that they participated in the *creation* of the law codes that governed their lives. For assessments of women's legal status during the period, see Christine Fell, *Women in Anglo-Saxon England* (Oxford: Blackwell, 1986); Elizabeth Judd, "Women before the Conquest: A Study of Women in Anglo-Saxon England," *Papers on Women's Studies* 1 (1974): 127–49; and Anne Klinck, "Anglo-Saxon Women and the Law," *Journal of Medieval History* 8 (1982): 107–22.

12. "About Chinese Women," 140.

13. This is not to say that there were no prominent religious women in Anglo-Saxon life and literature. However, religious heroines in Old English literature sacrifice their gender to succeed (see Jane Chance, *Woman as Hero in Old English Literature* [Syracuse: Syracuse University Press, 1986]), and, while the Anglo-Saxon church did offer aristocratic women a route to education and potential power, these women supported the patriarchal structure of the church.

An interesting gloss on gendered reading and on the "defeminizing" effect of the church emerges in the scholarly response to the correspondence of St. Boniface and is specifically relevant to this study. Both Peter Dronke and Christine Fell note similarities between the letters of Bertgyð and the Old English elegies discussed here, but Dronke (the man) compares the letters to *The Wife's Lament* and *Wulf and Eadwacer* "in the naked emotions expressed" (*Women Writers of the Middle Ages* [New York: Cambridge University Press, 1984], 31), while Fell (the woman) sees parallels to *The Wanderer* in Bertgyð's hope for final security with God: " 'where will be seen a perfect mansion, the land of the living, and the joy of angels rejoicing without end' " ("Some Implications of the Boniface Correspondence," *New Readings on Women in Old English Literature*, ed. Helen Damico and Alexandra Hennessey Olsen [Bloomington: Indiana University Press, 1990], 40). In the same article, Fell also places religious women more fully within the warrior class structure of Anglo-Saxon society: citing the laws of Ine of Wessex, Fell shows that an abbess could be the chosen *hlaford* of a traveller, with "the full responsibility for him as a member of her community" (31–32).

14. (New York: Columbia University Press, 1982).

15. Jacques Lacan, *Écrits*, trans. Alan Sheridan (New York: Norton, 1977), 103.

16. Jacques Lacan, "God and the *Jouissance* of The Woman," *Feminine Sexuality: Jacques Lacan and the école freudienne*, ed. Juliet Mitchell and Jacqueline Rose, trans. Jacqueline Rose (New York: Norton, 1985), 144.

17. *Écrits*, 68. In *Language, Sign, and Gender in* Beowulf, Overing argues for a similar asymmetry in the semiotic system of the Anglo-Saxons (see note 7).

18. Julia Kristeva, "Women's Time," *The Kristeva Reader*, 200. Hélène Cixous argues for the same kind of language in "The Laugh of the Medusa," *Signs* 1 (1976): 886.

19. Roman Jakobson, "Two Aspects of Language and Two Types of Aphasic Disturbances," *Language and Literature* (Cambridge: Harvard University Press, 1987), 98–99, 110.

20. Pat Belanoff's article "Women's Songs, Women's Language: *Wulf and Eadwacer* and *The Wife's Lament*" applies the theories of Kristeva, Cixous, and Luce Irigaray to *The Wife's Lament* and *Wulf and Eadwacer*, but Belanoff focuses on other features of the language, including the use of personal pronouns and the phrase structure (*New Readings*, 193–203).

21. For the conventional nature of silence, see Bjork.

22. For a discussion of the power of these women as speakers, see Barrie R. Straus, "Women's Words as Weapons: Speech as Action in 'The Wife's Lament'," *Texas Studies in Language and Literature* 23.2 (1981): 268–85; and Jane Chance, "The Errant Woman as *Scop* in *Wulf and Eadwacer* and *The Wife's Lament*," *Woman as Hero in Old English Literature*, 81–94.

On the Germanic tradition beginning with Tacitus which allows women greater freedom than men in expressing their emotions, especially grief, see "The Female Mourner at Beowulf's Funeral"; on the tradition of women as speakers of wisdom, see Fred C. Robinson, "The Prescient Woman in Old English Literature," *Philologia Anglica: Essays Presented to Professor Yoshio Terasawa on the Occasion of His Sixtieth Birthday* (Tokyo: Ken Kyusha, 1988), 240–50.

23. For a sampling of attempts at chronological reconstruction, see Jane L. Curry, "Approaches to a Translation of the Anglo-Saxon *Wife's Lament*," *MÆ* 35 (1966): 187–98; Thomas Davis, "Another View of *The Wife's Lament*," *PLL* 1 (1965): 291–305; R. P. Fitzgerald, "*The Wife's Lament* and the Search for the Lost Husband," *JEGP* 62 (1963): 769–77; Karl P. Wentersdorf, "The Situation of the Narrator in the OE *Wife's Lament*," *Speculum* 56 (1981): 492–516.

24. Exceptions are Rudolph C. Bambas, "Another View of *The Wife's Lament*," *JEGP* 62 (1963): 303–309; and Martin Stevens, "The Narrator of *The Wife's Lament*," *NM* 69 (1968): 72–90.

25. Marilyn Desmond questions the gender of "Anonymous," who wrote so much of our early literature, in "The Voice of Exile: Feminist Literary History and the Anonymous Anglo-Saxon Elegy," *Critical Inquiry* 16 (Spring 1990): 572–90. We can see how female sign interpreters have challenged patriarchal plot assumptions about the two poems in Marijane Osborn, "Text and Context of *Wulf and Eadwacer*," in *The Old English Elegies: New Essays in Criticism and Research*, ed. Martin Green (Rutherford: Fairleigh Dickinson University Press, 1983), 123–32, and Dolores Warwick Frese, "*Wulf and Eadwacer*: The Adulterous Woman Reconsidered," *Notre Dame English Journal* 15 (1983): 1–22. Both Osborn and Frese see a mother-son relationship as the focus of the poem, and not a woman torn between two lovers.

26. *Semiotic and Significs: The Correspondence between Charles Peirce and Victoria Lady Welby*, ed. Charles S. Hardwick (Bloomington: Indiana University Press, 1977), 111.

27. Charles S. Peirce, "Some Consequences of Four Incapacities," *Philosophical Writings of Peirce*, ed. Justus Buchler (New York: Dover, 1955), 247.

28. *The Sense of Grammar* (Bloomington: Indiana University Press, 1983), 17.

Class, Gender, Medieval Criticism, and *Piers Plowman*

✳ ✳ ✳

David Aers

Among the basic tasks of literary criticism, as I conceive it, is to discover what the maker of a text was up to in writing a particular work; and to understand the range of roles played by the text in the cultures where it circulated. These roles may or may not coincide with the writer's will and hopes. Whether they do or do not, all works necessarily take up "some determinate position in relation to some pre-existing conversation or argument."[1] Like the human beings who make them, they exist in what Charles Taylor has called "webs of interlocution."[2] We cannot hope to understand their identity, or that of their makers, without sustained attention to their communities and, where appropriate, to the groups against which their identity was defined. The need to pay attention to the construction and role of the 'other' needs emphasis in medieval literary studies because there we still find a tendency to abstract the unitary ambitions of prescriptive texts and then to project these as the maps to medieval culture, medieval piety, and 'the medieval mind'. What the projectors cannot see in their maps simply did not exist. Nor should we assume that such projectors are only found among those whose political assumptions and aspirations are of the 'right'.[3]

Among the concepts we need in our attempts to understand writings produced in those complex, heterogeneous communities we group as the Middle Ages are class and gender. We need many other concepts too, of course, but it is on these concepts that the present chapter focuses. We need these concepts as part, and 'part' needs stressing, of our attempt to understand the conditions of the social conversation, the 'web of interlocution' in which the texts we study were made and which they addressed. It "may indeed be impossible to recover more than a small fraction of the things" that a past writer was doing in a particular text. But, as Quentin Skinner argues, "the extent to which we can hope to understand'' the work, ''depends in part on the extent to which we can recover'' the things the writer was doing—to identify the questions and challenges to which the text is, in its own idioms, a response.[4]

In *Standards of Living in the Later Middle Ages,* Christopher Dyer observes that the ''enormous disparities between rich and poor'' were not the product of impersonal factors like climate, soil exhaustion, or microbes. They were the direct product of endowment and power networks which the concepts of class and gender enable us to identify and analyze. As he writes: ''The inequalities of the middle ages were not an incidental by-product of economic activity but an inherent feature of society. The great wealth of the aristocracy derived from their military, political and judicial domination of the subordinate peasantry. Services, goods and cash flowed upwards from the peasants to the Lords.''[5] Nor were extractions and the various mechanisms of extraction effected without coercion. And this coercion was confronted by widespread resistance, which took many forms. These forms ranged from symbolic ones, to actions such as the evasion of taxes and the non-performance of services, to poaching, to defiance of labor legislation, to, in the last resort, violence, whether hidden or in open riot. The English rising of 1381 was part of long-term struggles between classes, struggles which included contests over moral, social, and political values. In towns too, as Mervyn James and others have reminded us, pronouncements of 'social wholeness' and unity ''were in historical fact propagated by societies which were deeply divided,''[6] riven by a wide range of economic and political conflicts. No one is justified in ignoring all this. Nor are there good reasons for ignoring the heterogeneity in the role of Christianity in relation to the networks of power. John Ball, the Wyclifite preacher William White, and the lollard Hawisia Mone of Loddon were medieval Christians quite as much as John Gower, Archbishop Arundel, and Henry V.

The concept of class directs us to pay attention to forms of power involved in the organization of ''the extraction, transformation, distribution and consumption of the objects of nature.''[7] The concept directs us to consider, in Jon Elster's words, what ''people (in some sense) *have* to do'' rather than what they may choose to do. For example, there is a distinction between a gentleman who works on a farm or garden for pleasure or exercise and a person who works there out of economic necessity for wages or subsistence. (This is just the kind of distinction that is systematically excluded in new historicists' talk of 'social energy', 'exchange' and 'negotiation'.) Elster's own description of class, "in terms of endowments and behaviour," is as follows:

> The endowments include tangible property, intangible skills and more subtle cultural traits. The behaviours include working versus not working, selling versus buying labour-power, lending versus borrowing capital, renting versus hiring land, giving versus receiving commands in the management of corporate property . . . *A class is a group of people who by virtue of what they possess are compelled to engage in the same activities if they want to make the best use of their endowments.*[8]

Whether Elster's precise formulation is found persuasive or not, we certainly need some such concept of class to help us understand divisions and solidarities in and across medieval communities, and to grasp the ways in which the texts we study relate to these structures and the antagonisms they so often entailed. The concepts are certainly not to be applied in ways which dissolve the particularities of medieval forms of power, domination, and subordination. They must never be used reductively or as universal keys that make empirical study needless. On the contrary, they are heuristic, guides to our research, concepts which should bring to mind crucial areas of human experience which certain habits in the constitution of medieval literary studies have occluded.

What is true about the 'enormous disparities' produced through the organizations of social class is also true about the enormous disparities produced through the structural and ideological role of gender. Gender-identification produced massive inequalities within the same class and within the same social group. Detailed recent studies on this role of gender in the organization of work, wages, political power, and the distribution of resources within the same class, include outstanding work by Judith Bennett, Martha Howell, and Heather Swanson.[9] As with class, so with gender, we need to investigate the roles of Christianity in relation to given power structures, an investigation that medieval literary critics have been reluctant to pursue.

I have often argued that a reading of *Piers Plowman* carried out with complete blindness to class and class conflicts will misrepresent the force of certain areas of the poem even as it misrepresents the web of interlocutions to which it belongs. Langland's treatment of wasters, wage-laborers, the Statute of Labourers and resistance to it can serve as a good example. I have recently analyzed this area of the poem's treat-

ment of specific forces in a situation of class conflicts around determinate economic, political, and legal issues. Without conceptions of
class, networks of power, and the role of ideological legitimations of
particular material interests, a critic is likely to treat the passages in
question as satire against obvious cases of religious and moral delin-
quency.[10] This encourages the reader to remain unexaminedly within
the poet's own systems of representation. The result of such an unexamined procedure is that the terms of the poet's satire are not made the
subject of political and ethical analysis. On the contrary, they are naturalized. Consequently the critic can only address the human targets of
the poet's satire exclusively from within the poet's own terminology.
Indeed, it hardly occurs to such readers that their text may be taking up
a partisan line in a complex struggle between human beings. A critical
approach like this will elevate the poem's distinctly partial intervention
in a complex web of interlocutions and social conflicts into some universal and disinterested ethico-religious voice in the service of a putatively consensual understanding of justice and practical reason.

Such scholarship was evident in work on *Piers Plowman* published
in the 1980s. It can be represented by two books on the poem's politics and ethics, in which the ideological and fiercely partisan, class-
interested nature of the parliamentary laws and rhetoric around the
disputes was simply ignored. One scholar actually described the employers' self-interested wage-freeze and legislation as "fair terms,"
without even acknowledging that this might be disputable. This scholar
tells us that the Statutes of Labour were designed to enforce "loyalty
and honest work," to prevent "idleness," to "avert' hunger. We are
informed that the law was an "honest" one.[11] Yet these terms are actually judgments which assume a partisan alignment in a specific conflict between classes over resources, and, crucially, over the issue of
what should count as just relations between laborers and employers, between those who were obliged to sell their labor-power and those who
were the buyers and consumers of this commodity. Yet the medieval
literary scholar presents the judgments in question not as the political
ones they are but as indisputable and disinterested terms in some objective, transcendent ethical realm. This is simply not the case, for
terms like 'honest work', 'fair wages', and 'idleness' were terms whose
meanings were in contest, basic terms in a struggle between classes. It
will not do simply to assert: "We know that Piers is right to try to conform to the fourteenth-century labour laws."[12] Who is this "we" who
knows so confidently? Certainly it does not include the women and

men tried before justices throughout England for transgressing the labor legislation. And if the poem at this point encourages such a loaded use of the pronoun "we," as it does, if it encourages an uncritical alignment with the employers in this dispute, as it does, then *that* is precisely what a historical critic needs to focus on as a topic for reflection. Instead of simply reproducing the employers' position and self-legitimations, the critic needs to explore just how the "we" is produced, just whom it includes, just whom it excludes, and why. To assert that late fourteenth century laborers "generally preferred to abuse their new-found freedoms,"[13] is a striking example of *unacknowledged* political judgment passing itself off as value-free, and putatively objective historical criticism. This is encouraged by the scholar's failure to develop concepts of classes and the kind of attention such concepts can facilitate.

Another book published in the 1980s displayed a passionate identification with the line taken by the employing classes, a line which its author subsumed under universal justice. This critic asserted that all medieval readers would have found any challenge to "hierarchy" to be nothing but "an impious affront to the ordained order of the universe."[14] Impious, one supposes, because Christ is always assumed to support the economic legislation of all ruling classes in history? This would be a hard position to sustain in the face of the gospels' Jesus. Be that as it may, it is rather odd to claim that *all* medieval people had quite the modern scholar's confidence in the sanctity of precisely those forms of hierarchies that sought to rule and tax them. Let us think, for instance, of the widespread conflicts between many kinds of tenants and lords; between laborers and employers, laborers and justices; between laity and clerics; between Richard II's magnates and their king, a dispute culminating in the deposition and murder of the king in 1399, a deposition then legitimized in parliament. Let us think too of the 1381 rising, which included the execution of Archbishop Sudbury, and a widespread attack on the agents of 'justice'; think of the rebels' political and ethical projects, their sense of their own legitimacy. And let us think of the daily challenges to the supposedly 'ordained' hierarchy of gender relations, ones so memorably explored in the *Wife of Bath's Prologue* and so differently experienced in the *Book of Margery Kempe*.

We can only grasp the force and direction of Passus VI of *Piers Plowman*, only understand its minute particulars, when we see it as a politically committed piece of writing in a class struggle which many,

many English men and women experienced very differently to those who passed and tried to enforce the Statutes of Labour through coercive physical action, economic punishments, and rhetoric. Only if we grasp the ideological commitments at this point of the poem will we respond adequately to the famous turn in Passus VII where Piers abandons what has, in fact, been a disciplinary role in the service of particular vested interests. Indeed, the poet's *idealization* of such disciplinary action had been part of the problem. The greatness of *Piers Plowman* involves a deep and shifting ideological engagement with the communities, conflicts and webs of interlocution in late medieval England. No reading of the poem that turns its back on the networks of power, together with the conflicts they involved, can hope to meet the exploratory force, and difficulties, of the poem.

There is also a place for gender analysis in commentary on *Piers Plowman*. In my own view, a multi-track approach to the deployment of concepts of gender, race and class is necessary. It must be responsive to the particularities of the materials we address, responsive to the specificity of the networks and sources of power involved, and faithful to our own commitments. One obvious place where gender analysis is necessary in reading *Piers Plowman*, although this has not become normal yet in Langland studies, is in the case of Meed. The absence of attention to gender can actually distort even the most committedly historicist and political investigations of the poem. Such a historical reading of Meed is offered in Anna Baldwin's *The Theme of Government in* Piers Plowman. This scholarly and instructive study has become accepted as an authority in the areas of *Piers Plowman* it addresses, and the lack in its treatment of Meed is not at all unusual in Langland studies. This lack is witnessed in the way that James Simpson's outstanding study of *Piers Plowman*, published in 1990, devotes a chapter to Meed which has no concept of gender and, inevitably, no concern for the issues such a concept tends to bring into focus.[15]

Anna Baldwin argues that Yunck's work on venality satire, Meed, and what he called the "money economy" fails to "explain precisely what he [Langland] was attacking in his own society" (25).[16] In contrast, she tells us that her own chapter on Meed "will establish what she represents in contemporary life" (24). What Meed represents is the following: "a noblewoman" (25); "a personification of the evil noble" (25); "the nobility" (25); "the power of the nobility" (27); "the overpowerful noble" (33). The reading of this "personification" of "the power of the nobility" is developed in very close correlation to K. B.

McFarlane's account, and chronology, of "bastard feudalism."[17] Meed is read as the figure who represents the responsibility for creating 'indentures' in Langland's society (25–26). Quoting C III.263–67, Baldwin sees Meed "speaking as the creator of the indentured army, of which the late medieval retinues were a by-product" (36). And she insists: "Lady Meed did marshall the great indentured armies of Edward III" (36). Even on her first appearance, Meed "must have suggested to Langland's audience the lavish display of a great noble as well as the pervasive power of the purse" (27). The traditional link to Alice Perrers gets only a passing mention and is set aside (36). Instead the literary historian likens her to a powerful man, to Edward Courtenay, Earl of Devon, a comparison reiterated by James Simpson who here follows Anna Baldwin very closely, taking Meed as a satire on what he calls "the structures of 'bastard feudalism'."[18] This is precisely Anna Baldwin's sense of how she has managed to go beyond Yunck, allegedly bringing out the "real-life situation on which the allegory is modelled" (32), showing us how "in real medieval life" (31) Meed stands for "the over-powerful noble" in the "bastard feudalism" of the later fourteenth century. Langland's support for the King against this figure is taken as a sign of the poem's political stance, one that Anna Baldwin describes as proposing "absolutist ideas" enforced by "The triumph of absolutism in the poem as a whole," a triumph here foreshadowed by "an absolute monarch" representing the poet's "ideal of an absolutist monarch" (23, 55). While I continue to find *Piers Plowman* extremely resistant to any such 'absolutist' reading, for reasons that are to do with literary form and poetic modes as much as with explicit political arguments in the work, I do not intend to engage with that issue here. What I now wish to address is the issue of Meed's gender, an issue that will, obviously enough, only be made a topic for reflection if the critic's political and analytic vocabulary includes a concept of gender.

However instructive McFarlanesque accounts of late medieval England may be, they cannot answer at least one basic question. Namely, why would a poet represent as *female* the competitively masculine magnates of his society, the warrior honormen of the European wars and crusades, the ruling-class elite who were not only able to sustain its life-style by extracting rents, services, taxes and fines from the peasantry but also able to threaten the survival of monarchs whose policies they disliked?[19] Even Langland's exceptionally flexible and inventive allegorical modes could not readily have undertaken this task. Nor would there have seemed any need to represent competitive, militaristic magnates through a *feminine* figure. (He, like others, would have kept that feminizing figuration for knights and rulers who behaved in ways that were considered *un*manly, in *un*manly weakness and in an *un*manly lack of the aggressive disciplines considered appropriate for ruling class males, *mos feminarum*.) As for what Anna Baldwin calls "real medieval life," nothing could be less representative of its norms than having 'indentured' armies for foreign wars raised by a female figure. And it seems to me that we must not treat Meed's gender as transparent. It is crucial to Langland's purposes, a gendering through which he is figuring something other than the Earl of Devon and the magnates of McFarlane's "bastard feudalism." But before giving an account of why Langland needed a distinctively *feminine* figure in what is a distinctively misogynistic tradition of representation I will briefly draw attention to crucial areas that the concentration on "bastard feudalism" has obscured.

The first of these areas is the Church. Time and again, Meed's networks are unequivocally located in the agents, institutions, practices, and relationships of the Catholic Church. She is at home in its ordained officials, its lawyers, it distribution of benefices, its practice of the sacrament of penance (central in the poet's religious vision), and in its institutions from parish to papacy (for example, C II.19–24, 175–93; III.21–67, 178–88, 270–78).[20] Furthermore, we are given the memorable example of Meed herself at confession, receiving a financial penance and absolution from a friar whose spiritual work is determined by the exchange economy he inhabits. One cannot sideline this emphasis by stating that ecclesiastical practice "does not interfere with the government of the *kingdom*" (Baldwin, 28). Such a move to split off religion from politics and social justice is quite alien to *Piers Plowman*. Such a splitting off is, in fact, more the product of post-Enlightenment and officially secularized societies; for Langland what happens in the Church has serious consequences not only for individual salvation but for the whole community in a range of interlocking activities. It is perfectly logical, within the terms of Langland's vision, to maintain, as Liberum Arbitrium does in C XVI, that if the Church and its priesthood is in sin, the whole people and the community is heading for catastrophe (XVI.271–83). It is surely not by chance that the figure who brings Meed into definition as the one who negates Christian teaching in all institutions, from pope's palace to king's court and law-enforcement agencies (C II.5–24), is Holy Church. Nor is it by chance that Meed is challenged by Theology, who attempts to initiate a reformation in Passus II (116–54).

The second area to consider here is that of small-scale urban commodity production, one whose significance in *Piers Plowman* I have addressed before.[21] Anna Baldwin notes that while this seems not to be directly related to "bastard feudalism" it is nevertheless an example of how Meed "collects some borough officials in order to make life in London easier for her friends and retainers" (30). Yet the poet's own attention is bestowed on those who produce and control the exchange of commodities on which the poor, "þe mene peple," are dependent— "bakeres and breweres, bocheres and cokes," those who "Rychen thorw regraterye and rentes hem beggeth" (III.77–126). These retail traders, the poet maintains, are able to exploit "the peple þat parselmele mot begge" (III.86). The elaboration of the B-version here includes an attack on the urban patriciate for colluding in this state of affairs for financial gain (III.108–14). The third area is the representation of Meed as a bad exegete (III.482–97). This aspect of Langland's figuration is bound up with her *gender*, for her gender, as we shall see, becomes a marker of the carnal and self-interested interpretation of texts—just as much as the Wife of Bath's is.[22] This takes me into the fourth area—the prominence given to Meed's overflowing sexuality. This is inextricably bound up with the construction of the feminine in the misogynistic traditions with which all medievalists are very familiar. These four areas of representation must not be marginalized in any reading of Meed. They indicate that she is a figure whose meaning far exceeds anything that could be called "bastard feudalism," indeed, that she is designed to address a set of concerns which do not even coincide with features that are specific to the politics of McFarlane's "bastard feudalism."

In thinking about Meed it seems best to begin with the question Clare Lees has put in the present volume: how is she *produced?* Certainly she is produced in answer to the male dreamer's *desire*—his desire to know the false (II.4). Now one could easily imagine answering a question about falsity with the figure of, say, Judas Iscariot . . . or of one taken from the male elites of the fourteenth century at the heart of McFarlane's "bastard feudalism." But Langland rejected all such possibilities and chose, on the left hand side of course, "a womman . . . wonderly yclothed," a woman who, as Clare Lees emphasizes, is all *appearance* and whose appearance "raveschede my herte" (II.5–16). The dreamer's ravishment leads immediately to his concern with what man she belongs to: "Whos wyf a were" (II.17). The figure's *gender* in relation to a male dreamer and male poet is basic to Meed's production and significance.

True enough, at this moment she has an aristocratic appearance.[23] Yet even this aristocratic appearance is *only* appearance, a product of her array at this initial moment of Will's desire. For as much as being the figure of a courtly lady she is represented as the figure of the *common prostitute*. Not only is she an Alice Perrers available to the rulers of the world, she is explicitly presented as, for example, a 'baud', one who is a trickster of words and an open body:

> tikel of here tayl, talewys of tonge,
> As comyn as þe cartway to knaues and to all
> (III.166–67)

Indeed, the poet stresses that her body is available to learned and to unlearned, to lepers in the hedges and, in his own words, "to alle men" (III.160–69). This is no Earl of Devon.

Once one introduces the category of gender it becomes clear that the poet has composed the figure of Meed by organizing the standard components of the 'feminine' in the male-authored gender system of his culture. We can recall how in that culture 'femininity' is consistently identified with carnality and the letter, with perversity, garrulousness, fickleness, and verbal trickery. Even those female figures who escape this grid are defined through it—as exceptions, such as the Blessed Virgin Mary and saints, or secular analogues like Chaucer's Blanche. As Howard Bloch noted in his study of medieval misogyny, the 'feminine' in this discourse represents "the other" which threatens the "masculine" and against which the masculine is defined; in Bloch's deconstructionist vocabulary, it is the "supplemental," the "secondary," the "illusory" and all that threatens the "proper" meaning of texts.[24] In fact, the 'feminine' represents the carnal in all its senses, and that is why the poet includes the bad exegete in the figure's attributes. More to my present concerns, that is precisely why she represents for the poet just what Yunck long ago claimed she did: an economy in which production and exchange are determined by profit. For Langland the profit economy he saw pervading social relations and spiritual relations was the source and embodiment of much he detested and feared in his own search for a just and stable community responsive to the call of Christ. This is why her identity includes that of noblewoman, courtly lady, ecclesiastic patroness, representative of the arms industry, representative of small-scale commodity production and the exploitation of those without property and capital resources, representative of the urban patriciate; and also a common prostitute. She is a female body constantly open to all men, the product of male fantasy that produces such figures across the centuries, both an object of desire and an object of fear and contempt.

Langland insists on the image of the common prostitute while deploying that drearily commonplace pun: "þe comune calde here queynte comune hore" (IV.161: see too III.164–69). In thinking about the fusion of economic nexus and gender in Meed, it is worth recalling R. I. Moore's comments on prostitution in his fascinating study *The Formation of a Persecuting Society:*

> Prostitution . . . is not only essentially an urban phenomenon, but necessarily a cash-based one; indeed, the relationship between the prostitute and her client could serve as a paradigm of the anxiety so widely expressed in these centuries [i.e., *eleventh* and *twelfth*] that money dissolved traditional personal ties and obligations and substituted for them impersonal one-way transactions which contributed nothing to the maintenance and renewal of the social fabric.[25]

As a number of recent studies have shown, by Langland's time prostitution had become a profitable institution for urban and courtly entrepreneurs in a system of licensing, monopolies, and rents to which the Church gave ideological and practical legitimation.[26] It would be a gross mistake to join those literary critics who assume that markets and production for exchange value, so prominent in Langland's visions, were a radical innovation in his lifetime. On the contrary, the period of most marked intensive and extensive growth in markets, towns, and a money-economy was the twelfth and thirteenth centuries, as the work of so many historians has made plain.[27] The fact that we never see Meed taking money from men did not make the poet qualify his classification of her as a prostitute because the prostitute is the *symbol* he wanted for a voracious, ever-open, all-consuming sexual body, one which flows everywhere and is fixed nowhere. "As comyn as þe cartway," he writes, showing that she, like Death, makes no distinctions between lepers, knaves, priests, sheriffs, and earls. Her pervasive pres-

ence opens all closed doors and dissolves all apparently fixed and trust-
worthy forms, her gender and sexuality symbolizing this work. No
wonder she is the perfect symbol for the poet's vision of the effects of
an economy in which, as the Wife of Bath and her maker knew, "all is
for to sell."[28]

So unlike Yunck and unlike more recent Langland scholars, we need
the concept of gender if we are to understand just how and just why this
economic and cultural nexus should be produced as feminine. Without
the concept of gender the critic will naturalize what he or she reads,
failing to notice that there is anything here to explain at all. The literature on *Piers Plowman* certainly witnesses to this, for right up to the
present time, and even in the work of distinguished scholars, we find an
inability to ask why a particular form of economic production and
exchange should be gendered as it is, why it should be represented
as feminine.

In conclusion I wish to suggest that the absence of the concept of
gender here has further consequences. It blinds us to the obstacles the
decision creates for the poet's attempt to grasp the nature of the practices he wishes to transform: the choice to feminize the exchange economy encouraged simplifications and evasions of the very problems he
addressed with such intensity. It also encourages readers to substitute
identification with the text's system of representation and judgment for
critical inquiry, a tendency that is neither desirable in itself nor one encouraged by the great, exploratory poem that can still draw our attention and passion across the centuries.

Gender analysis from a variety of perspectives has now become pervasive in Chaucer studies. In that field, class analysis has also made
contributions to our understanding of the poet's formal strategies and
his political vision. Can such analysis be relevant to explicitly devo-
tional and instructional texts in Christian traditions? My own work on
class and gender in the formation of Margery Kempe's identity, a basically dual-track approach, shows that my answer is an unequivocal
affirmative.[29] But some medievalists seem to disagree *in principle* with
this project. As far as I understand them, they think that someone trying to analyze the role of class, gender, race, economic contexts, and
political interests in the form and function of religious texts must have
abandoned the quest for historical understanding. The charge, according to a collection of essays published in 1990, is that such criticism is
disqualified by its "decidedly post-medieval standards."[30] Such
charges tend to make certain assumptions. It is assumed that the scholar

making them does, in fact, work with distinctively 'medieval' concepts, critical criteria, and values. It is also assumed that someone whose so-called 'standards' (I would prefer the term 'critical paradigms') are 'non-medieval' is *necessarily* failing to make any contribution to historical analysis of medieval texts and culture. A further assumption often goes with this accusation of 'non-medieval standards', and the editor of the collection in question makes it very explicit: that those whose critical practice is objected to *must* be Marxists, humanists, and materialists. Here my response to these assumptions is necessarily brief. First, for a modern writer of any critical, political, or religious persuasion to claim that she or he has achieved (if that is the appropriate term) 'medieval standards', that is, an authentically medieval worldview, is based on considerable self-deception. It simply fails to acknowledge the inevitable presence of the knower and her or his horizons in the known. This inevitability has been the subject of profound study within modern hermeneutic traditions and it is certainly one that fascinated Chaucer—as Judith Ferster has shown.[31]

Traditions in the sociology of knowledge are also relevant here. Our attempt to gain historical understanding is carried out within paradigms and horizons that are our own, grounded in our own traditions, our own specific ways of raising questions, and so of addressing issues. The quality of historical understanding is not enhanced by a denial of our own historical contingency and the way this present shapes us all. Another factor also needs to be remembered, once again, in the face of such comfortably homogenizing talk about 'medieval standards': medieval communities and ideas were neither homogeneous nor unitary and such invocations of 'medieval standards' tend to forget that in some crucial areas these were both contested and changing. Ball, Usk, Chaucer, Wyclif, and Badby, in their different ways, all had good cause to ask with Ancient Pistol, "Under which king, besonian? Speak, or die." Three of these, of course, spoke *and* died, their words unacceptable to the power that counted. And one of them had the remains of his body dug up and ritually desecrated for his words, words unacceptable to the leaders of the church. Such memories of the interactions between language, life, and death may remind us that the works we study did not, and do not, only relate to other writings. They also related, and may still relate, to human lives and deaths, to peoples' explorations of the possibilities and consequences of various forms of life. What we read can also affect our imaginations and knowledge, contributing to our formation of desires, our vision of human possibilities, our senses of self and others. So the works we read are engaged, time and again, with a question that we have now been taught not to address—at least if we want recognition as competent critics, theorists, and literary historians: how should we live? Our texts often have designs upon us, include dimensions that are inescapably moral and involve our engagement not only as centers of pleasure and gamesomeness but as moral beings, ones who may even be seriously concerned with that old, recurring question, how should we live? We should recollect that if there were some such entity as 'medieval standards', and it were to be propagated by a medieval text, then any response to it, past or present, would include an ethical moment and ethical choices—including decisions about how to read and in what contexts to situate what we read . . . and teach. So we should not let any talk about 'medieval standards' persuade us to obliterate the distinction between the understanding of works made in a past culture and the desire to identify with certain sentiments and ideas held by its members—or at least those of its members whom the scholar selects for consideration. The consequences of such a failure are hardly propitious. For example, it would entail that a critic who studies Nazi Germany, and wishes not to be judged 'anachronistic' or 'elitist' or unhistorical, must reject all analytic concepts of class, gender, and race which do not reproduce the 'standards', representations, and ideas prevalent in official Nazi culture and in the popular culture to which it appealed. It would also entail sympathetic identification with the Nazi ideologues we were studying. This involves a morally repugnant understanding of that past society and culture, of the collective actions it sponsored and legitimized. Are medievalists unusually prone to take the identification with past sentiments and ideas as historical analysis? If so, why?

The third assumption especially interests me: that those whose explorations of medieval religion include the concepts of class and gender must be dismissed as Marxists, humanists, and materialists (especially culpable examples of 'non-medieval' paradigms). Here it is worth observing that some medievalists seem to confuse historical materialism with ontological materialism. They tend to assume that those who have special concern "to examine political power" in religious writing "are oblivious to the operation of spiritual power,"[32] to assume that a real concern with Christian spirituality could not possibly make one particularly interested in analyzing the roles and effects of political powers (including those stemming from divisions of gender, class, and race) within the constitution of spiritual domains, including the institutions and discourses whose end is precisely to minister to the spirit. Yet why should anyone think this? I am quite certain that both the Catholic poet Langland and the great and radical Protestant poet Milton held just such a fusion of interests, and that such concerns were not at all marginal to their poetry. On a basic aspect of the issue here, the theologian who is currently the Anglican Bishop of Durham has observed that "the claims of the church and the churches have to be subjected to all the valid insights of a Marx or a Freud or a Durkheim. It is as plain as a pikestaff, as Marx said, that religion is again and again used in the interests of the ruling classes."[33] And it would be in accord with his work to take "ruling classes" here to include men's systematic lordship over women and to make use of relevant insights and analysis of gender-formation from within feminist traditions—including those of feminist theology. Nothing in what I am saying, of course, necessitates the abandonment of scrupulous historical study and the commitments to historical understanding with which this chapter opened.

Finally, I suggest we settle without anxiety for whatever conceptualizations help us to knowledge about networks of power in medieval culture, their sources and effects. This is an essential part of studying the formation of specific human and textual identities. We can never know *a priori* precisely what combination of concepts are likely to prove most fruitful in analyzing a particular text or community. All we can do is seek to learn what we can about available conceptualizations of the sources of power (gender, class, race, ideology, military, economy . . .) . . . and learn, as we go along, their limitations in the face of that which confronts us. We need always to treat them as heuristic guides in our inquiries. And, perhaps, certain medievalists especially need to think about the Bishop of Durham's appeal that we be "critical of the spirit of *this* age," but equally "critical of the spirit of *past* ages."[34] Those who have a genuine concern with Christian spirituality have no cause to abandon scrupulous inquiry into the political and economic relationships of Christian writings and practices, both past and present. Far from being an eloquent testimony of faith, such an abandonment of critical inquiry into its political, social, and economic relationships seems to me more a sign of anxiety, of a fearfulness that was, at least, quite alien to the critical explorations of Langland and many, many late medieval Christians, both orthodox and heterodox.

Notes

1. See *Meaning and Context: Quentin Skinner and his Critics,* ed. James Tully (Cambridge: Polity, 1988), 274; chapter 14 is especially relevant here.

2. Charles Taylor, *Sources of the Self* (Cambridge: Cambridge University Press, 1989), 36.

3. For reflections on convergences between self-styled radical work and the most overtly conservative medievalism, see David Aers, chapter 6 in *Culture and History, 1350–1600,* ed. Aers (Hemel Hempstead: Harvester, 1992).

4. Skinner, *Meaning and Context,* 262–63.

5. C. Dyer, *Standards of Living in the Later Middle Ages* (Oxford: Oxford University Press, 1990), 6.

6. M. James, "Ritual, drama and the social body in the late medieval English town," *Past and Present* 98 (1983): 3–29; see references and comments in David Aers, *Community, Gender and Individual Identity in English Writing, 1360–1430* (London: Routledge, 1988), 9–10, 181.

7. Quoting Michael Mann, *The Sources of Social Power* (Cambridge: Cambridge University Press, 1986), 24.

8. Jon Elster, *Making Sense of Marx* (Cambridge: Cambridge University Press, 1985), 324, 330–31.

9. Judith Bennett, *Women in the Medieval English Countryside* (New York: Oxford University Press, 1986); Martha Howell, *Women, Production, and Patriarchy in Late Medieval Cities* (Chicago: University of Chicago Press, 1985); Heather Swanson, *Medieval Artisans* (Oxford: Blackwell, 1989); Judith Bennett et al., eds., *Sisters and Workers in the Middle Ages* (Chicago: University of Chicago Press, 1989). The literature in this area is substantial and increasing impressively: literary critics will find much here to sustain their attention and to help them historicize their conceptualizations of gender and power.

10. Aers, *Community and Gender,* chapter 1. A popular alternative has been to allegorize the whole episode, treating all agricultural discourse as reference to commonplaces in Christian doctrine and pastoral exhortation. I argued against this approach in Piers Plowman *and Christian Allegory* (London: Arnold, 1975); but it persists, however bizarre the consequences—for a recent example, Pamela Raabe, *Imitating God: The Allegory of Faith in* Piers Plowman *B* (Athens: University of Georgia Press, 1990), 135.

11. Anna P. Baldwin, *The Theme of Government in* Piers Plowman (Cambridge: Brewer, 1981), *seriatim,* 58, 57, 60, 59.

12. Baldwin, *Theme,* 59.

13. Baldwin, *Theme,* 82.

14. M. Stokes, *Justice and Mercy in* Piers Plowman (London: Croom Helm, 1984), 211; see 201, 210–12.

15. Baldwin, *Theme* (page references to this work hereafter given in the text); James Simpson, Piers Plowman: *An Introduction to the B-Text* (London: Longman, 1990), chapter 2.

16. John Yunck, *The Lineage of Lady Meed* (Notre Dame: University of Notre Dame Press, 1963).

17. For an important historical reflection on McFarlane's concept of "bastard-feudalism," and his chronology, see P. Coss, "Bastard-feudalism revised," *Past and Present* 125 (1989): 27–64. This article should be read by those literary historians who apply McFarlane's work as an authority free from serious problems.

18. Simpson, Piers Plowman, 51.

19. On 'honourmen' see M. James, *English Politics and the Concept of Honour* (London: Past and Present Society, 1978); and M. Keen, *Chivalry* (New Haven: Yale University Press, 1984).

20. In this chapter I refer to the edition of the C version of *Piers Plowman,* ed. Derek Pearsall (London: Arnold, 1978). The C version is the one addressed by Baldwin in her own study of the poem.

21. Aers, *Chaucer, Langland and the Creative Imagination* (London: Routledge, 1980), 6–11.

22. On the issues here, Carolyn Dinshaw, *Chaucer's Sexual Poetics* (Madison: University of Wisconsin Press, 1989), introduction and chapter 1.

23. Predictably enough, many commentators feel free to read her as the apocalyptic woman in purple and scarlet with a gold cup in her hand and seated on many waters (Revelations, 17); they do so, however, only by dissolving the specificities and carefully drawn boundaries of Langland's own iconography.

24. H. Bloch, "Medieval Misogyny," *Representations* 20 (1987): 1–24.

25. R. I. Moore, *The Formation of a Persecuting Society* (Oxford: Blackwell, 1987), 95.

26. See, for example, Leah L. Otis, *Prostitution in Medieval Society* (Chicago: University of Chicago Press, 1985); J. Rossiaud, *Medieval Prostitution* (Oxford: Blackwell, 1988); J. Richards, *Sex, Dissidence and Damnations: Minority Groups in the Middle Ages* (London: Routledge, 1991), chapter 6, on prostitutes; Bronislaw Geremek, *The Margins of Society in Late Medieval Paris* (Cambridge: Cambridge University Press, 1987), chapter 7 on the "world of prostitution."

27. See references in Aers, *Community and Gender,* 12–16.

28. *Wife of Bath's Prologue,* 1.414, in *The Works of Geoffrey Chaucer* (Riverside edition, Oxford: Oxford University Press, 1989).

29. Aers, *Community and Gender,* chapter 2.

30. C. D. Benson and E. Robertson, *Chaucer's Religious Tales* (Cambridge: Brewer, 1990), quoting here from 5.

31. J. Ferster, *Chaucer on Interpretation* (Cambridge: Cambridge University Press, 1985); see too Lee Patterson, *Negotiating the Past* (Madison: University of Wisconsin Press, 1987), chapter 1; basic to the argument here is the work of H. G. Gadamer, *Truth and Method* (London: Sheed and Ward, 1975); Paul Ricoeur, *Hermeneutics and the Human Sciences* (Cambridge: Cambridge University Press, 1981), and Charles Taylor, *Philosophy and the Human Sciences* (Cambridge: Cambridge University Press, 1985), especially chapters 1 and 2.

32. Benson and Robertson, *Chaucer's Religious Tales,* 5.

33. David Jenkins, *God, Miracles and the Church of England* (London: SCM, 1987), 15.

34. Jenkins, *God,* 99.

Construction of Class, Family, and Gender in Some Middle English Popular Romances

✽ ✽ ✽

Harriet E. Hudson

The subjects of this chapter are four English romances from the late Middle Ages: *Sir Eglamour of Artois* (ca. 1350), *Torrent of Portengale* (ca. 1400), *Paris and Vienne* (1478), and *The Squire of Low Degree* (ca. 1500).[1] Today obscure, these narratives once enjoyed fair popularity. *Eglamour* survives in several manuscripts (six), and all the narratives saw multiple printings through the 1600s. Their heroes and heroines are referred to in contemporaneous literary works, as well as in records of dramatic performances. These romances tell much the same story: a lesser knight wins his lord's daughter in marriage, only to be separated from her through treachery and regain her through perseverance. Their treatment of this plot is formulaic: the narratives embody traditional elements shared by many Middle English popular romances. The doubled exile-and-return (separation-and-reunion) episodes and the calumniated queen motif will be familiar to readers of these narratives. What is distinctive about the present four is the way they manipulate their formulaic material so as to explore conflicting ideas about social class, family, and gender.

The narratives are structurally homologous, and, initially, practically identical. However, the later romances present a different working out of the conflicts arising from the lovers' betrothal. After receiving his lady's and her father's assent to his suit, and accomplishing the designated tasks, Eglamour becomes betrothed to Cristabelle privately. They consummate their union before the knight departs to perform his final test. When a son is born, her father declares him illegitimate and casts daughter and child adrift. The lovers are eventually reunited; the couple celebrate their marriage and reclaim their patrimony while the lady's father is killed. In later romances there is no clandestine marriage; the couples remain chaste, so no children are born; the daughters are imprisoned rather than exiled; and eventually they are reconciled with their fathers. All the narratives, however, raise the same vexed questions about hereditary social status and the power of patriarchy, the complexity of which may be belied by the stories' conventional happy endings, but was almost certainly not lost on medieval audiences.

What follows is an examination of constructions of social class, gender, and family as accomplished by the four romances and as practiced by their audiences. Of particular interest is the way the narratives minimize and make compatible several fundamental contradictions existing in gentle society of late medieval England. These may be phrased as a series of issues: whether social status should be determined by lineage or self-assertion; whether wealth should circulate through primogeniture or enterprise; whether worthiness derives from ancestry or individual virtue; whether power may be wielded by women in a patriarchal society. Concerns about gender, class, and family are brought to a crux in the romances' depiction of father-daughter conflict over control of marriage. In his study of the changing marriage patterns of early modern Europe, Alan MacFarlane cites as evidence the "enormous amount" of discussion devoted to questions of control over marriage in Elizabethan, Jacobean, and Restoration drama.[2] I think we can see earlier evidence of this discussion in the romances under consideration; and, I suggest, the differences between the fourteenth- and fifteenth-century narratives can be associated with changes in ideologies of class and gender accompanying the slow shift from medieval to recognizably modern systems of class and family. These ideological changes correlate with several other cultural trends: the formation of a gentry class much concerned with aggrandizement of property and social advancement of family through marriage, the emergence of a family dynamic of affective individualism at the expense of hierarchical (patriarchal) authority, and the modification of canon law to limit individuals' autonomy in matrimony.

Before proceeding with my discussion, I should comment on the gentry audience assumed by my approach. To generalize about a complex topic, Middle English popular romances reached a diverse audience, depending on the occasion of their reading or recitation, and were produced in diverse milieux.[3] However, they are particularly associated with the gentry. Many manuscripts containing romances, including those of the present four, were owned by members of the gentry or haute bourgeoisie. The degree to which these people saw romance-reading as an assertion of status is well illustrated by the anonymous lament for John Berkeley, a Leicestershire knight of the late fourteenth century. He is praised for his chivalry and generosity as a host, with whom one could spend the day hunting or reading romances in the company of fair damsels—a very model of gentility.[4]

The situation of the lovers in our four romances lends itself to conflicting constructions of social status because the suitor belongs to a social rank inferior to that of his beloved. Indeed, this is the factor that would seem to precipitate the main conflict of the stories. Susan Wittig demonstrates how the romances address their audiences' concerns about the restrictiveness of their social system by mediating contradictory ideologies. In analyzing the deep structures of male-Cinderella romances like *Eglamour,* she explains that they offer the hope of upward mobility to worthy men of lower status while simultaneously suggesting "that worth and birth are synonymous, that only a gentleman can be a gentle man."[5] These positions are articulated in a dialogue between Eglamour and his squire. The more hierarchical and conservative point of view is expressed by the squire:

> Ye ar a knyt of lyttyll lond:
> Take not to euyll, I vndirstond.
>   For mykyll wolde haue more.
> If I went to that lady and told her so,
> Peraunter on skorn take hit wold scho
>   And lyghtly lett me fare.
> Syr, a mon that hewyth oeyr hye
> Lyghtly the chyppus fallen in hiss eye—
>   Thus happis hyt ofte aywhare.
>
> Syr, bethinke the of this thinge:
> Ther wowes here emperor and kynge
>   And dukes that are bolde;
> Erles, barouns and knyghts also—
> Yitt wyll sche none of al tho
>   But euur in goodnes herr hold.
> Sche wold neuer a kyng forsake
> And a sympull knyght take,
>   Butt yif your lufe wer olde.
> I swere by God, heuen Kynge,
> Wyste her fadyr of sych a thyng
>   Full dere hytt scholde be solde. (64–84)[6]

Here the concern is for lack of land (income), low rank, and paternal wrath. The proverbial expressions, embodiments of accepted cultural wisdom, stress that those who already have much would have still more, and that those who overreach cause their own discomfiture.

Eglamour's response to his squire is couched in terms, not of possessions and rank, but of personal, chivalric excellence:

> "My sqwyer, sethen thou was a chylde
>   Thow hast ben lened with me:
> In dede of armes, in many a stowre,
> Wher saw thou euur my dyshonowre?
>   Sey on, so God saue the!"
> "Nay, syr, by Ihesu bryght!
> Ye are on of the noblest knyghts
>   That ys knowen in cristyante:
> In dede of armes, by God on lyue,
> Ye are counted worth othur fyve!" (86–95)

These are the very qualities which recommend Eglamour to the earl's favor:

> He hath serued vs many a day,
> Full trewly in hys entent—
> In iustyng and in turnament
> He seyde vs neuyr nay.
> In dede of armes, wher he myght here,
> He wynnes the gree with iurnay clere,
>   My worschyp euyer and ay. (125–30)

Cristabelle, too, refers to his loyalty and valor when she accepts his suit:

> And euer trewe vndur thy schylde
> Thou wynnes the gre in euery fylde,
>   Worschypfully, be the rode. (160–63)

She also mentions that he is "comen of gentyll blode" (159). Thus Eglamour is of gentle status as well as manner; his lack of great estates seems unimportant to father and daughter.

The Squire of Low Degree deals explicitly with matters of social advancement, in keeping with the class-consciousness of its usual title and the fact that its hero has no proper name. The King of Hungary is remarkably encouraging of social mobility:

> I have sene that many a page
> Have become men by mariage;
> Than it is semely that squier
> To have my doughter by this manere,
> And eche man in his degree
> Become a lorde of royalty,
> By fortune and by other grace,
> By heritage and by purchase. (373–80)

> If he be so poore of fame
> That ye may not be wedded for shame
> Bring him to me anone right.
> I shall make him squire and knight.
> And if he be so great a lorde
> That your love may not accord
> Let me, doughter, that lording see;
> He shall have golde ynough with thee. (725–33)[7]

Here one is not fixed on social rank but may move up or down in status. One may move up by good fortune, that is, a grant of lands or position from a patron; by inheritance, including bequests from outside the immediate family; and by purchase, a practice that was becoming common in the fifteenth century when *The Squire* was written.[8] The monetary basis of status is reiterated in this romance by its frequent use of the formula "gold and fee." *The Squire* is an extreme example of the tendency, common in Middle English romances, to "open up" the *récit clos* of the French narratives that were their sources and analogues.[9] As Susan Crane has demonstrated in her examination of Insular romance, the conventional discourse of the English poems eschews exclusivity, touting instead the accessibility and imitability of chivalry and courtly love. The romances devote much attention to objects and activities of class display: armor, combats, tournaments, hunting, feasting.

In contrast to the Hungarian king's liberal outlook, the Dauphin of Vienne's is more conservative. Perhaps the disparity in the lover's social status is more of an impediment in *Paris and Vienne* because the romance is French and originated in courtly, not gentry circles. Paris himself says it is folly to declare his love to Vienne, since he is a man of "lytel estate." The parents on both sides consider such an unequal match an outrage against protocol and social order—despite the fact that Paris's father is "a noble man of ancyent lygnage and of fayr londes and was wel beloued of the daulphyn & of alle thye lordes of the lande" (2).[10]

The differing social ideas espoused by the characters of the romances are all implicit in the gentry ethos. By a complex process of descent from the older baronage, development of urban and administrative occupations, and multiplication and stratification of social ranks, the gentry had emerged as a distinct class toward the end of the Middle Ages.[11] In the early years of the fourteenth century, the baronage was undifferentiated from landowners whose holdings were worth twenty pounds a year in rents (a knight's fee). In the fifteenth century there was a fivefold peerage and threefold grouping of gentles—that is, knights, esquires, and gentlemen.[12] The designations corresponded loosely to income differentials, though twenty pounds remained a knight's fee, as Chaucer's social-climbing Franklin was well aware.[13] While there were no rigid barriers between gentry and peerage, and intermarriage was possible, there would have been a real difference in kind between the nobles, who had an assured identity in lineage, an entailed title, and nonpartible estates, and the gentry, who had no titles to convey in marriage and whose estates fragmented and refocused as they were formed.[14] As estate administration or household service for the great was the coveted employment of the gentry, their relationship to the peerage was often one of dependence.[15] To sum up in the words of Kenneth McFarlane, by the fifteenth century "nobility had parted company with gentility, the quality with which those rejected were still permitted to be endowed."[16] In so doing, they set the stage for the *gentilesse* debate, so memorably set forth in the Wife of Bath's fairy-tale romance. Ultimately, gentility remained a matter of self-assertion and was thus different from knighthood, which required dubbing, and a title, which depended on royal grant.[17] The social self-consciousness arising in such circumstances led to a quickening of social aspirations and anxiety and an age characterized by "ambition and upward striving."[18]

Family aggrandizement preoccupied the gentry. Detailed regional studies of the English gentry reveal an obsessive concern for the preservation and extension of property and the advancement of family through marriage.[19] Indeed, A. J. Pollard says marriage was the most important social institution and custom binding the gentry together.[20] According to Carol Rawcliffe, members of the nobility and gentry planned the marriages of their children with the interests of future generations in mind; that is, long-term dynastic gains, not immediate cash profits.[21] Christine Carpenter's analysis of fifteenth-century Warwickshire gentry shows that neither nobility nor gentry acquired estates by purchase if they could avoid it; rather, they preferred to marry into them.[22]

Thus family relations and social status are inextricably linked in the gentry ethos. Our romances' concern for family matters may be related to a trend described by social historians—the shift from a lineal concept of family and a dynamic of deference and distance to an affective individualism that increased the importance of the nuclear family and close personal relationships among family members. Lawrence Stone finds this shift most pronounced among families of the gentry and professional classes; they were on the leading edge of the value change.[23] However, the change was only beginning in the late Middle Ages, and the family dynamics of the gentry were generally characterized by patrilineage and primogeniture.[24] These practices gave great importance to one's family affiliation while making close relationships with family members difficult to maintain. Family was important as lineage, as determiner of social status, not as a group of individuals. Gentry spouses were frequently separated in the administration of far-flung estates and performance of government service. The custom of sending children to serve and be fostered in the households of others (usually with an eye to social advantage) is widely documented. Though Stone's hypothesis that medieval parents had little affection for their children has been challenged, many gentry families may have had few opportunities to form strong personal bonds.

The interests of lineage frequently ran counter to the interests of individual family members, especially children and females, so certain conflicts seem to have been built into the system. Gentry families are defined very narrowly in bequests. Younger brothers usually got bequests of goods (not lands), daughters got dowries. As Carpenter states, aptly for our purposes, "the great majority of these families were just not rich enough to support a wider kin group or to leave younger sons with much more than the hope, nurtured by their fairy-tale counterparts, of finding a rich princess."[25] Another fantasy of younger sons was to overcome their brothers. However, even the eldest son was disadvantaged as long as his father lived, though he might prosper through marriage to an heiress. Stone found that heirs of squires often married only at their fathers' deaths, suggesting that they could not claim full status, or were not able to support a family independently of their parents, while their fathers lived—a situation bound to produce conflicts.[26]

It is tempting to see some relationship between all this and the appearance in fourteenth-century England of a new type of romance that concerned family conflict. Lee Ramsey calls them domestic romances, observing that in them family relationships are greatly valued, but are not close, largely because the greatest threats to the family are seen to come from within the family.[27] In our romances, lineage is preserved but family members are often absent from and unknown to each other. In all but *Paris and Vienne,* the hero has no living relatives. The plots are built around such taboos as incest, prenuptial sex, illegitimacy, patricide, and infanticide—a heightened figuring of the gentry reality. Threats of incest and other taboos are more pronounced in earlier romances; the later ones have a tendency to diffuse such matters. *Eglamour* is one of only two Middle English popular romances in which an incestuous marriage to the mother actually takes place (the other is *Degaré*). The son, separated from his mother in infancy, unwittingly wins her hand in a tournament, but his identity is discovered before the marriage is consummated and the union is declared null. The narrator makes sure the incest does not go unrecognized by the audience, reminding us "his owen mother has he wed," and "they were sybbe full nere." *Torrent,* which often follows *Eglamour* closely, avoids suggestions of incest. The reunion episode is a joust analogous to the one in *Eglamour,* but it is nowhere made explicit that the victor is expected to marry the lady, and she recognizes Torrent before the dilemma of marrying her own son is ever really presented.

Similar threats to the family are posed by patricide. Fathers and sons fight unrecognized in the tournaments that reunite the family, though no lives are lost—the fathers either prevail or fight to a draw. The heroines' fathers do not fare so well; in both *Torrent* and *Eglamour* they are killed, vindicating the lovers. When Torrent returns to discover the emperor's treachery, he has him set adrift to die—thus acting out the suitor's fantasy of killing his bride's father. Since Cristabelle's father dies in a providential fall from a tower (where he cowardly flees as Eglamour approaches), the knight is saved the necessity of murdering the father and the mechanism of the formula is shifted from human revenge to divine providence.

In the earlier, three-generation romances, family conflicts are resolved only by eliminating generations. The older generation of block-
ing fathers is killed off; the potentially threatening younger generation
of sons is adopted out. Eglamour's and Torrent's sons are found and
raised by childless royalty who make them their heirs; after they return
to their rightful patrimony to celebrate their parents' marriage, the sons
go to their adoptive kingdoms and live independently of their parents.
These fortuitous circumstances eliminate a major cause of father-son
conflict but do not address the real problem: the practice of delayed inheritance to preserve the power of the father.

The authority of the fathers is undermined by their own treachery in
Eglamour and *Torrent*. Both fathers pledge assent to their daughters'
marriages before witnesses and then do all in their power to prevent
them. They obviously intend the young men to be killed in the performance of their tests and curse them as diabolical when they return tri-
umphant. Only the intercession of the court prevents Eglamour's earl
from sending him immediately on his third test in spite of the knight's
request for time to recuperate from his wounds. In *Torrent*, the emper-
or's wife and his whole court turn against him when he plans another
marriage for his daughter, then exiles her. Further, they support Torrent
in setting the emperor adrift. The father's actual motive for thwarting
the union seems to be simple jealousy—his daughter is too good for
any suitor, he wants to keep her for himself—which is not far removed
from the incestuous fathers of the similarly structured romances, *Apol-
lonius of Tyre* and *Emaré*.

In the later romances, *Paris and Vienne* and *The Squire*, the authority
of the father is affirmed rather than questioned. Neither father breaks
troth, and both live. The King of Hungary is a very powerful figure, an
orchestrator who, in fact, controls all the action: he allows the steward
to try to expose the lovers, he withholds from his daughter the knowledge that the Squire survived the combat with the steward, and allows
her to persist in her mourning while he sends the Squire on his quests.
He does test the lovers' constancy, but the princess immures herself by
becoming a recluse; she is not imprisoned. Rather than punishing his
daughter, the king offers her various delights and blandishments to
cheer her, a dilemma almost opposite to Vienne's deprivation. The father actually brings about the lovers' reunion. Vienne's father is less
favorably portrayed. Though he is not treacherous, he is relentless in
his persecution of his daughter and Paris's family. Perhaps his cruelty
would have been considered commensurate with his daughter's trans-

gression in eloping. If in *Eglamour* and *Torrent* the lovers' transgression is a form of sexual incontinence, in *Paris and Vienne* it is defiance of parental authority. Vienne is very aware of the seriousness of her offense against patriarchy and is constantly reminded of it by others.

Paris and Vienne neatly reverses the usual formulas of patricide. Rather than in any sense killing the dauphin, Paris saves his life. When the dauphin is captured by the infidel, Paris, disguised as a Moslem, frees him, and in gratitude the dauphin offers Vienne to his young benefactor. After she has recognized Paris, he reveals his identity to the dauphin and is married to his lady with her father's full blessings. Instead of ending as treacherous outcasts of family and society, the later fathers are reconciled in their families' reunions.

The constant in our romances' representations of family dynamics is the generational conflict over control of marriage. The romances vindicate the younger generation and marriage based on personal emotional attachment rather than on familial or social obligation. The ideology of marriage for love's sake prevails, in the case of the hero and heroine, and is validated by their ascent to power—a neat negotiation of a synthesis with the dominant ideology of marriage for status' sake. In practice, the project of family aggrandizement through patrilineage demanded that marriages be carefully controlled. However, individual temperaments and the ideology of romantic love threatened that control, valuing conjugal relationships above all others.[28] The gentry recognized the importance of compatibility and the advantages of personal attraction in the success of a union, but these were not a primary concern. Keith Dockray notes that to some extent the matter of choice depended on a family's style and strategy in marrying its offspring.[29] The gentry frequently arranged marriages for their minor children, though social commentators ridiculed the practice; Dockray and Rawcliffe have speculated that there was very little room for choice on the part of the couple in most gentry marriages.[30] Generally boys had more autonomy in arranging their espousals than did their sisters, and some eldest sons had great autonomy.[31] This was the case in the Paston family. When certain Paston women asserted their right to choose, however, the consequences were confinement, beating, and ostracism, even legal action, though ultimately, their choices prevailed. Compared to theirs, Vienne's ordeal seems nothing extraordinary.

The question of control over marriage had legal and ecclesiastical aspects as well as familial and social ones. R. H. Helmholtz's study of medieval English marriage litigation reveals that, in court records surviving from the fourteenth century, over ninety percent of the cases concerning matrimony related to questions of clandestine marriage.[32] Gratian's *Concordance of Discordant Canons* declared that a valid marriage was constituted when the lovers consented to their union and spoke words to that effect. Strictly defined, the words spoken by the lovers alone, without benefit of banns, witnesses, or clergy, constituted a legitimate, binding union, indeed, a sacrament.[33] Canonists considered marriage from the couple's point of view, says Michael Sheehan.[34] According to Noonan, Gratian "recognized the place of individualistic, unsocial decision-making in the choice of spouses."[35] The law's insistence on the free consent of the couple and the equality of the sexes in constituting the union was, in theory at least, empowering to women. This conception of marriage based upon private, individualistic considerations evaded institutional authority: MacFarlane finds that "neither church nor feudal lord nor family could supply the . . . [necessary] . . . element of emotion-colored assent."[36] The law also weakened the permanence of marriage which the church sought to establish, since an individual could easily disregard a secret union if he or she desired to wed another. The interpretation thwarted the interests of lineage since the family had no necessary role in arranging the marriage, and the union could produce heirs of questionable legitimacy from spouses of inferior status.

The Church's response to the situation was formulated by the Fourth Lateran Council, which declared private marriages to be clandestine, and thus punishable, though not invalid. Readings of banns were required, as well as the participation of priests. Gradually, in its attempt to root out clandestine marriages, the Church prescribed a more public and protracted chain of events through which the marriage was made. Finally, in the sixteenth century, as marriage law came under the jurisdiction of civil, not ecclesiastical, authorities, the Council of Trent dictated that clandestine marriages were invalid. If early Church statutes enhanced the personal nature of consent, later ones enhanced control by a wider circle providing publicity for the marriage and a public memory of its existence.[37] These changes, which also went against vestiges of Germanic custom, no doubt contributed to the preponderance of legal cases involving clandestine marriage discovered by Helmholtz.

When we consider the changes in marriage law, it is perhaps not surprising that the early romances' betrothals constitute a legitimate union, while the later ones are constituted only in public ceremony. All the romances are concerned to establish that the lovers are, in a sense, married. In all but *Paris and Vienne*, the fathers initially assent to the union. Torrent and his lady are publicly betrothed, with the empress's and the court's express approval, as the emperor sets the wedding date. After they privately exchange vows of betrothal and sleep together, Eglamour gives a ring to Cristabelle and the unborn child, and dowries to her ladies who pledge loyalty to the couple. In both *Eglamour* and *Torrent* betrothals are consummated without condemnation, perhaps further evidence that authors and audiences understood their unions as legitimate.[38]

In an important shift, virginity in the later romances takes on much the same significance that consummation has in the earlier ones; that is, it further validates the couple's union. Vienne is scrupulous about the matter: one of her conditions for eloping with Paris is that "ye touchest not my body vnto the time that we be lawfully maryed" (34), and arrangements are made for her and her lady-in-waiting Isabeau to sleep apart from the men, with a chaperone. The heroine has the men who return her to her father report to him that she is "pure and clean of her body" (41); and later she, Isabeau, and the chaplain who sheltered them attest to this as well. These statements, we are told, secretly please the dauphin. In *The Squire,* though the treacherous steward tries to prove the couple are lovers, the princess vows to maintain her virginity for the Squire, and later, when she thinks him dead, for all Christian men.

This emphasis on virginity accords with the social and ecclesiastical pressures which finally made clandestine marriage invalid. Over the course of the Middle Ages, the ecclesiastical ideal of celibacy influenced the values of those committed to the active life. The valorization of virginity also furthered the aims of patriarchy and patrilineage, eliminating the problem of illegitimacy. While a woman's virginity was at all times regarded by her family as a precious commodity, evidence suggests that, in the mid-Tudor period, consummation before solemnization was less common than earlier and loss of virginity in such circumstances was considered to dishonor the woman.[39] Vienne recognizes the relationship of virginity to control of women and decides to take control of it herself, as she does of other situations. Do we have here some seeds of the later Renaissance fascination with virginity used so adeptly by the Virgin Queen?

The structurally analogous but contradictory states, virginity and motherhood, result in imprisonment or exile, which are also analogous but contradictory. The virgins are restricted: bound by family, physically restrained within the family dwelling, they are stationary and separate from the world. Exiles are expelled from the family to wander in the great world like their lost lovers. In theory, a married woman and her children belonged to her husband's family, having left her own family behind. Illegitimate children, too, were cut off from their families, or at least their patrimonies. An unmarried woman, on the other hand, was very much the possession of her parents or guardians, and virginity could best be protected by close supervision and restriction.

Though exile and imprisonment in the romances should be understood in terms of the family dynamics of the later Middle Ages, they also have analogues in religious literature. The exiled heroines of such pious legends as *Constance* and *Florence of Rome* belong to the tradition of calumniated queens. The exile's journey, which in our romances brings the protagonists to the Holy Land, was a metaphor for the condition of humankind and an analogue to pilgrimage and crusade. Vienne's steadfast resistance in prison reminds one of the virgin martyrs of the Katherine Group of saints' lives. The Squire's lady, following a more passive model, becomes a recluse to venerate the memory of her lover and considers taking the veil. The cult of relics is suggested by the princess's enshrinement of what she believes to be the Squire's mutilated head (it is actually the steward's).

The status of our heroines as mothers or virgins is less significant than their status as a ruler's only heir.[40] Vienne's and the Princess of Hungary's names are synonymous with their patrimonies. All the suitors are expressly to be awarded the father's titles and lands upon marriage to the daughters. Such situations jeopardized the patrimony of ranking families but offered others the opportunity to marry into that patrimony; thus they had both a positive and a negative valence. Even when a woman was not a lone heiress, the pressure to marry off daughters, to settle them independently of the patrimony, made marriages to men of lesser rank but suitable means acceptable. Though such men might not gain great wealth, their progeny would carry the woman's superior blood, which determined social status. In her role as heiress and conveyor of the gentle blood, the heroine is the key to identity in the recognition and reunion scenes of the early romances. She is the one who reconstitutes the family, recognizing the man's identity from the scenes depicted by his armorial bearings. The heroines of the later romances have lost this function. In *The Squire*, the father is the key to identity, and in *Paris and Vienne*, it is Paris himself who produces the ring Vienne had given him long before. But then the heroines of the later romances have no children, generate no lineage to identify.

Ramsey and other scholars suggest that women would have been attracted to these romances by their empowered heroines.[41] Certainly the romances devote much attention to the heroines, following their vicissitudes with the same attention given to those of their lovers. In *The Squire*, the princess is actually the focus of the story; her lover's combats and journeys are reported indirectly and only briefly in the character's conversations. Vienne is clever and assertive. Making good use of the Church's teaching, she insists in speech after speech that a marriage without both individuals' consent is not legitimate. She then uses the fact that she has consented to Paris, and refuses consent to any other suitor, as an effective impediment to her father's coercion. It is Vienne who arranges the first meeting with her lover; she tells Paris they must marry, and when her father refuses assent, she tells Paris to plan their elopement. She even chides her despondent lover when they are discovered and invents the grotesque ruse by which she is able to avoid her father's pressures to marry. The odor of the rotting chicken she conceals in her armpits convinces all suitors that she is too diseased to marry.[42]

This greater attention to women in the romances occurs at a time when the legal and marital power of women was apparently diminishing. To speak in general terms, since there were more women than men in the marriage market of urban and noble classes, the main burdens of marriage began to fall on women and their families; they paid large dowries and financed the wedding.[43] Laws limited women's abilities to acquire property through marriage, keep property in marriage, or grant landholdings to their husbands. David Herlihy suggests such changes were related to the decline in importance of women as administrators of estates and the proliferation of professional administrators.[44] While this was true among the nobility (the old barony), it was less true of the gentry, who often were the professional administrators for the nobility and had to administer their own eagerly acquired estates as well. Haskell shows that this was a major function of English gentry women, pointing out that the characters of women revealed in Paston, Stonor, and Plumpton correspondence are practical individuals of real social and economic power.[45] Capable women with administrative talents were important to the success of a gentry family. Heroines in the romances have social and economic power as heiresses, not as administrators of estates, but like their real-life counterparts, they exercise power within the frameworks of patriarchal systems.

Ultimately, our romances try to have it both ways, maintaining the contradictory principles inherent in the gentry's position: personal worth (understood as *gentilesse*) is a function of lineage, personal worth is a function of individual achievement; social status and property are inherited, status and property may be acquired independently of birth; family lineage is important, relationships with family members are not close; marriage is an instrument of power, marriage is an expression of love. The romances seem to synthesize upward social mobility with an undervaluation of kinship, while continuing to associate high status with lineage. They are able to negotiate this and other uneasy apparent syntheses because the terms are functions of different systems: upward mobility is associated with a proto-capitalism; undervalued kinship with primogeniture and gender struggle within patriarchal feudalism.

To some extent, the formulas of romance are subversive: they question the authority of parents and lords while affirming the authority of the individual and love for its own sake. On the other hand, this love renews the family and re-establishes the same social order. The romances are empowering to females, members of the younger generation, and those of lesser rank, but only within the terms of power recognized by patriarchy. It is only men who are upwardly mobile in these and most other romances. (Upwardly mobile women are more often found in exemplary genres, where, like Griselda, they serve as models of Christian humility.) The later romances are less subversive than the earlier: they do not deal in taboos like incest and patricide, the families remain intact, the position of fathers is enhanced, and marriages are consummated only after they have been publicly celebrated with parental approval and church ceremony. Women still choose their own marriage partner, and suitors of lesser status still marry heiresses; but they do so with less destructiveness to the family. By simultaneously entertaining incompatible constructions of gender and class, the romances validate the very structures they seem to threaten, and conveniently obscure, in the careers of their characters, the fundamental contradictions shaping the lives and self-concepts of their audiences.

Notes

1. *Eglamour* (1335 lines) and *Torrent* (2668 lines) were composed in tail-rhyme stanzas in the northeast Midlands. The latter is a reworking of the Eglamour plot, expanded by multiplication of the stock episodes already present. *The Squire of Low Degree* (1132 lines) employs couplets which had (again) become fashionable for romances in the fifteenth century. It devotes many passages to "courtly" description, and at times seems self-consciously Chaucerian in its rhetoric, though it also uses the formulaic language of the tail-rhyme romances. *Paris and Vienne*, a prose romance, is much longer than the poems, and more realistic than they. Also in contrast to the poems, which are anonymous and originated in England, *Paris and Vienne* was composed (1432) by Pierre la Cypede, an officer in the Duke of Burgundy's establishment at Marseilles. Printed in an abridged version, this was translated and published by William Caxton in 1478. Though it originated in a different cultural milieu and literary tradition, in the sixteenth century it would have reached much the same English audience as the indigenous romances. All were printed by Wynken de Worde.

2. Alan MacFarlane, *Marriage and Love in England 1300–1840* (Oxford: Blackwell, 1986), 143.

3. Derek Pearsall comments on this diversity in "The Audiences of the Middle English Romances," *Historical and Editorial Studies in Medieval and Early Modern English for Johan Gerritsen*, ed. Mary-Jo Arn and Hanneke Wirtjes (Groningen: Wolters-Noordhoff, 1985), 37–47. Knights like Robert Thornton owned copies of *Eglamour* (Lincoln Cathedral ms. 91); the proprietress of a London inn lent a romance of Guy of Warwick to the Paston family, who also owned a book from Caxton's press; John Colyns, a prominent London guildsman, had a copy of *Ipomedon*—Richard III owned another version. Romances were read aloud in the owners' domestic circle, performed for bishops in their chambers, and recited to mixed audiences at public entertainments and great feasts which brought together the inhabitants of a manor and its dependencies. Production by clerks, whether in households of gentry and nobles, or in ecclesiastical establishments was common.

4. Thorlac Turville-Petre prints the lament in "Lament for John Berkeley," *Speculum* 57 (1982): 332–39; see also "Some English Manuscripts in the North-East Midlands," *Manuscripts and Readers in Fifteenth-Century England*, ed. Derek Pearsall (Cambridge: Boydell and Brewer, 1983), 126.

5. Susan Wittig, *Stylistic and Narrative Structures in the Middle English Romances* (Austin: University of Texas Press, 1978), 189.

6. *Sir Eglamour of Artois*, ed. Frances Richardson, EETS 256 (London: Oxford University Press, 1965).

7. "The Squire of Low Degree," *Middle English Verse Romances*, ed. Donald Sands (New York: Holt, Rinehart, Winston, 1966), 249–78.

8. The aristocratic purchase of land was a relatively new thing in the fifteenth century; earlier it had changed hands mainly by inheritance or royal grant. See Christine Carpenter, "The Fifteenth-Century English Gentry and

Their Estates,'' *Gentry and Lesser Nobility in Late Medieval Europe*, ed. Michael Jones (New York: St. Martins, 1986), 44.

9. Susan Crane, *Insular Romance* (Berkeley: University of California Press, 1986), 211, relates this opening up to the development of the English barony as distinct from the continental French *noblesse*.

10. William Caxton, *Paris and Vienne*, ed. MacEdward Leach, EETS 234 (London: Oxford University Press, 1957).

11. N. Denholm-Young, *The Country Gentry in the Fourteenth Century* (Oxford: Clarendon, 1969).

12. D. A. L. Morgan, ''The Individual Style of the English Gentleman,'' in *Gentry and Lesser Nobility in Late Medieval Europe*, ed. Michael Jones (New York: St. Martins, 1986), 16.

13. Geoffrey Chaucer, *The Canterbury Tales*, ed. John H. Fisher, 2nd ed. (New York: Holt, Rinehart, Winston, 1989) V.683.

14. Carpenter, 54.

15. A. J. Pollard, ''The Richmondshire Community of Gentry during the Wars of the Roses,'' in *Patronage, Pedigree and Power in Later Medieval England*, ed. Charles Ross (London: Sutton, Rowman, Littlefield, 1979), 48. Morgan, 26.

16. Kenneth B. McFarlane, *The Nobility of Later Medieval England* (Oxford: Clarendon, 1973), 275.

17. Morgan, 8.

18. George R. Keiser, ''Lincoln Cathedral Library ms. 91: Life and Milieu of the Scribe,'' *Studies in Bibliography* 32 (1979): 158, draws upon F. R. H. Du Boulay's *An Age of Ambition: English Society in the Late Middle Ages* in describing the social milieu of Robert Thornton, who copied a text of *Eglamour*.

19. Carol Rawcliffe, ''The Politics of Marriage in Later Medieval England: William Lord Botreaux and the Hungerfords,'' *Huntington Library Quarterly* 51 (1988): 170.

20. Pollard, 47.

21. Rawcliffe, 163.

22. Carpenter, 38.

23. Lawrence Stone, *The Family, Sex, and Marriage in England 1500–1800* (New York: Harper, 1977), 10.

24. F. R. H. Du Boulay, in *The Lordship of Canterbury: An Essay on Medieval Society* (London: Nelson, 1966), indicates that in Kent, families continued to find ways to exercise primogeniture though the laws forbade a parent to leave his entire estate to only one of several children.

25. Carpenter, 52.

26. Stone, 46.

27. Lee Ramsey, *Chivalric Romances: Popular Literature in Medieval England* (Bloomington: Indiana University Press, 1986), 158. The differences between these domestic romances and earlier romances of very similar structure can be seen in the examples of Horn and Havelok—both orphaned princes who regain their patrimonies and assert right rule in their countries. The heroes of the domestic romances are knights who marry into patrimony and establish a family. Also see Stephen Knight, ''The Social Function of the Middle English

Romances," in *Medieval Literature,* ed. David Aers (New York: St. Martins, 1986), 99–122.

28. MacFarlane, 131.

29. Keith Dockray, "Why Did Fifteenth-Century English Gentry Marry?: The Pastons, Plumptons and Stonors Reconsidered," in *Gentry and Lesser Nobility in Late Medieval Europe,* ed. Michael Jones (New York: St. Martins, 1986), 64–68.

30. MacFarlane cites instances of criticism, 133; Dockray, 68; Rawcliffe, 163. Ralph Houlbrook says that among the middle classes, the individual choice of the couple was the usual basis for matrimony ("The Making of Marriage in Mid-Tudor England: Evidence from the Records of Matrimonial Contract Litigation," *Journal of Family History* 10 [1985]: 339). See also Michael Sheehan, "Choice of Marriage Partner in the Middle Ages: The Development and Application of a Theory of Marriage," *Medieval and Renaissance History* n.s. 1 (1978): 3–33.

31. Ann S. Haskell, "The Paston Women on Marriage in Fifteenth Century England," *Viator* 4 (1973): 467.

32. R. H. Helmholtz, *Marriage Litigation in Medieval England* (Cambridge: Cambridge University Press, 1974), 30.

33. According to canon law, words spoken *de presenti,* that is, in the present tense, constituted a marriage (since it was thought that in the exchange of words, the couple mutually endowed each other with the sacrament). Something on the order of "You are my husband" or "I take you as my wife" would suffice. Words spoken *de futuro,* that is, "I will marry you" or "I will be your husband," accompanied by intercourse, also constituted a marriage. It is no wonder that so much of the litigation concerning marriages in late medieval England centered on questions of validity. In part, Helmholtz attributes this preponderance to the fact that Church law interpreted *verba de presenti* as a complete marriage while many people regarded them as a contract to marry; marriage was complete with solemnization and consummation (31). There had long been a tradition of private marriage contract among Germanic peoples. See also Zacharias Thundy, "Clandestine Marriages in the Late Middle Ages," in *New Images of Medieval Women: Essays toward a Cultural Anthropology,* ed. Edelgard E. Du Bruck (Lewiston, NY: Mellen, 1989), 304–20.

The marriage of mother and son inverts the terms of her earlier marriage to Eglamour. The incestuous marriage, which is duly celebrated, is invalid, while the lovers' union, which is uncelebrated, is legitimate. The incestuous marriage is easily annulled once the couple's true relationship is known.

34. Michael M. Sheehan, "The Formation and Stability of Marriage in Fourteenth Century England: Evidence of an Ely Register," *Medieval Studies* 33 (1971): 229.

35. John T. Noonan, Jr., "Power to Choose," *Viator* 4 (1973): 423.

36. MacFarlane, 121.

37. Michael M. Sheehan, "Marriage Theory and Practice in the Conciliar Legislation and Diocesan Statutes of Medieval England," *Medieval Studies* 40 (1975): 458.

38. In a similar situation, the lovers in *Amis and Amiloun* are condemned by a heavenly voice and exposed by a jealous steward. Diether Mehl notes the op-

eration of divine providence in the couple's eventual triumph and the rarity of genuinely illegitimate births in Middle English romances, but does not explore the nature of the parents' union (*The Middle English Romances of the Thirteenth and Fourteenth Centuries* [London: Routledge and Kegan Paul, 1967], 179). Edmund Reiss suggests that the nearly fatal wound Eglamour receives from the dragon of Rome and the separation from Cristabelle are punishments for his immoral behavior ("Romance," in *The Popular Literature of Medieval England*, ed. Thomas Heffernan, Tennessee Studies in Literature 28 [Knoxville: University of Tennessee Press, 1985], 124). Frances Richardson, in a note (p. 114), indicates that the lovers in *Eglamour* would have been considered married under canon law; so the audience would have rejected the Earl's charges of illegitimacy.

39. Haskell, 468; Houlbrook, 339.

40. The heroine's mother plays a role in *Torrent* and *Paris and Vienne;* in *Eglamour* and *The Squire* she is deceased and her absence contributes to fragmentation of family. In some similar romances, for example, *Emaré*, the death of the mother leaves the daughter exposed to the father's lust. When mothers are present, they support their daughter's choice of husband and remonstrate with their own husband on the harshness of his treatment of the daughter; but they can not sway their spouse from his course of action.

41. Ramsey, 157; also William Cotton, "Fidelity, Suffering and Humor in Caxton's *Paris and Vienne*," *Chivalric Literature*, ed. Larry D. Benson and John Leyerle, Studies in Medieval Culture xiv (Kalamazoo: Medieval Institute Publications, 1980), 96.

42. Thus purity is maintained by the appearance of filth, moral integrity by the appearance of physical corruption. Marvelously, Paris is not repelled by the stench, but finds it sweet.

43. Eglamour's gift of dowries to Cristabelle's ladies should be seen in light of these circumstances. David Herlihy explains that the giving of dowries to dependent or impoverished girls was regarded as an act of Christian charity. See *Medieval Households* (Cambridge: Harvard University Press, 1985), 98.

44. Ibid., 100.

45. Haskell, 460.

Building Class and Gender into Chaucer's *Hous*

* * *

Britton J. Harwood

Aristocrats and peasants, and the burghers who deal with them from the towns, are—as poetry peculiarly insists—always male and female. Gender is no less a basic fact about people, past or present, than economic or political agency. In economic discourse, gender may be, as Cora Kaplan asserts, "mystified, presented in ideological form." And "traditional Marxist thought" has no doubt taken the oppression of women to be self-evident and thus in no need of analysis.[1] But fiction insists on the irreducibility of the genders and the history of their struggle.[2] A materialist criticism aiming to avoid that reduction therefore faces the task of theorizing a relation between what, in turn, are two further sets of relations.[3] Class and gender and their importance for the production and consumption of texts have often been taken up independently of each other. Attempts to describe the nature and extent of their interdependence have been less frequent.

Such attempts might well develop Heidi Hartmann's notion that "Marxist methodology *can* be used to formulate feminist strategy. . . ."[4] Specifically, I wish to propose that, as Marxist methodology has been developed by Louis Althusser and his students, it is not tied exclusively to the determinations of a struggle between economic classes. To the contrary, it can clarify gender conflict. Perhaps the most promising way to avoid the naturalization of gender is to think of the emergence of gender by analogy with the emergence of class.[5] Classes do not first exist and then fight to acquire or keep a surplus. Rather, "separate individuals form a class only insofar as they have to carry on a common battle against another class."[6] Classes are not the cause but the consequence of conflict over the surplus product—the use values produced by labor additional to the products necessary for reproducing labor.

The nature of this analogy between gender and class will be seen if we begin with Engels's point that biological reproduction—engendering in one sense—reproduces "immediate life" in one way, just as making the means of existence (food, clothing, and the like) does in another.[7] The two (re)productions do not reduce to each other, of course. If it seems silly to put a child, the object of so much psychological investment, in the same sentence with ten pounds of yarn (or any other example of the surplus product), every use value, in its own degree, is an object of desire; and tending a child and carding wool are both purposeful expenditures of energy ("abstract labor"). Gender arises and individuals become en-gendered in the course of struggle for the child. And just as the yarn is also labor (alienated labor when the yarn is viewed as the capitalist's private property), so is the baby. Thus, gender struggle is not simply the effort to control fertility or otherwise "own" the product. (Chaucer's father, for example, was abducted by his own paternal aunt.)[8] It is the effort to extend (or to prevent the extension of) parturient labor into child care and all the domestic services culturally linked to it. Accordingly, Michèle Barrett writes about the distinctive character of gender struggle when she concludes that "the possibility of women's liberation lies crucially in a re-allocation of childcare. . . ."[9]

If the contests of class and gender are irreducible to each other, then a superstructure can be expected to exist for each of these bases, relatively autonomous from the base in each case and acting reciprocally upon it. One set of politico-legal and ideological "levels" or "instances" will be determined "in the last instance" by, and will act upon, the structure of classes;[10] another set will be comparably related to the structure of genders. In each case the superstructure will seek to secure the structure "below," always with the proviso that each instance is itself the site of conflict. For example, a kinship system is a political if not legal means of acting upon gender relations. When the avunculate tie gave way in the post-Carolingian age "to the agnatic bias,"[11] then the mother's position in relation to the child (who had formerly inherited through his maternal uncle) would seem to have been weakened in favor of the father's.

The reproductive effect upon gender relations of any particular (politico-legal) institution, such as a law court, can be distinguished from its function, at the same or some other time, in securing the class structure. For example, "*women's* contentiousness" was singled out for correction in "special, enlarged sessions" of the *curia* of Battle

Abbey. In that same court, the beadle might be ordered to seize the chattels of customary tenants in order to compel them to perform labor services that were owing the lord of the manor.[12] The existence of a single institution—a manorial court, for instance—at the political level does not entail an identity of class and gender conflict at the base. Because of an institutional history and needs of its own, an apparatus that was political, or ideological, or both might at any time have had even contradictory effects upon the family: the eventual view of the Church that a bride and groom needed only to express their consent in order to marry undermined a paternal authority that the Church in other ways sustained.[13] And individuals served their interests with decisions that ramified within both sets of relations. The virgater who put a high premium on child labor (and the prospect of the larger surplus for the market that this additional labor made possible) remained in the fields while his wife partially withdrew "at frequent intervals to procreate and care for infants."[14] Dynastic lineage, using the entailment of estates from about 1300 to prevent the alienation and division of land, reinforced the dependent status of women at the same time it served the amassing of ever larger properties.

Because poets, like critics, write from positions within history, their work inevitably intervenes in the contests of class and gender.[15] Such positions are defined in the defense of them. To illustrate one possible articulation of a criticism of class with one of gender, I shall devote the remainder of this chapter to Chaucer's *Hous of Fame,* pointing to its reproductive force. Following Pierre Macherey, I want to call these defenses Chaucer's "ideological project," but always with the recognition that the poem as a project of ideology is also determined by literary convention.

This follows because a writer has two different operations. "The project of writing begins inevitably by taking the form of an ideological imperative"; but this project "will have to adopt the conditions of the possibility of such an undertaking." Specifically, the ideological project can exist only as a project of writing. When it therefore takes up the means of expression, these "do not appear instantaneously" for the writer "but at the end of a long history" of texts. Writing, that is, while never ceasing to elaborate ideological themes, has a history of its own, one that cannot be appropriated intact, because the writer is impelled by the exigencies of a certain moment.[16] On the one hand, ideology remains an alien presence in the text, which exists within particular textual histories. On the other, like an unconscious utterance, this alien

presence does not cease to speak, to interfere; and it does so most of all
in its distortions (in the neutral sense of 'changes') of the expressive
means—its distortions of textual history. Thus we might begin with
how the literary tradition of *fama* obviously changes in Chaucer's poem
and then try to explain some of this in light of a certain ideological
pressure.

If Ovid's description of *Fama* in Book 12 of the *Metamorphoses* is
the seed of the *Hous of Fame*, then Chaucer clearly adds to this description. But he also divides it. He adds a synopsis of the *Aeneid*, di-
lating the story of Dido; he writes at length on the nature of sound; he
amplifies *Fama* as *Fortuna*, whom he calls her sister (1547), thus making Fame's inconstancy her most memorable feature; and finally, Chaucer supplements the castle of Fame with a wicker house full of
tidings.[17] This addition, however, is actually a division. In the words of
the late J. A. W. Bennett, as Chaucer "bisects the classical . . . concept of *Fama* into 'Fame' and 'Rumour,' so he bisects Ovid's description, reserving for the house of twigs the features that in Ovid pertain
to [Fame's] house of sounding brass."[18] The location of the dwelling of
Fama in Ovid, on a mountaintop, in the midst of land, sea, and sky
(12.39–40), is assigned by Chaucer to the castle (714–15).[19] The thousand holes on the roof of *Fama*'s dwelling (12.44), however, are assigned to the wicker house (1948–49). Ovid's comparisons of the noise
of *Fama* to distant waves or the last rumbling of thunder (12.50–52) are
borrowed for the "grete soun" from the castle (1025, 1027), where
true and false are intermixed (1029) as in Ovid (12.54–55). Chaucer
assigns Ovid's throngs of people (12.53), however, to the wicker house
(2034-42), describing the castle, by contrast, as uncrowded (1358–59).
And he similarly assigns to the wicker house the phenomenon that stories grow in size, as each teller adds a contribution (*Met.* 12.57–58; *HF*
2059–75).

We can begin to explain these changes by noting that the poem forges
one link between masculinity and effective activity, another between
women and suffering. For the moment I would like to leave Fame herself out of account. If we do, then men of "gret auctorite" (2158)
frame the poem—Macrobius and Virgil at the beginning, some other
great *auctor* where the poem leaves off. An *auctor* literally augments,
gives increase. Men in this poem give it in writing, which, with the
exception of the names chiseled in ice under the auspices of Fame, is
associated with metal and permanence.[20] The poem as a whole attacks
oral transmission and sides with writing. What Virgil writes *about*,

however, is Dido, with *auctoritas* and permanence surrounding and positioning a vulnerable woman. Recently, Elaine Tuttle Hansen has described the *Hous of Fame* as "a male poet's dream of enabling and storyworthy discourse, that is grounded in and takes off from its concern to fix the reputation of a (dead) woman. Dido . . . is brought to imaginative life and made into a speaking subject in Book I of the poem, but then she is forgotten, left behind, and killed off. In suicide, she confirms her proper sense of shame. . . ."[21] Virtually *all* women disappear from the poem with Dido. Men survive and always control. Specific events are in the hands of St. Leonard, Synon, Pyrrhus, Aeneas, Demophon, Achilles, the anonymous fellow who burnt the temple of Isis, and preeminently the eagle, who begins neuter in gender but turns promptly and permanently masculine. With the single exception of Dianira, who kills Hercules, what women can do in this poem is first to fall in love and then to kill themselves. Otherwise, they ask, pray, and complain.

Now I want to reintroduce the lady Fame, but by way of the house of twigs. As if it were perched on Mt. Athos, there is not so much as a feminine pronoun in this domicile. What happens there is that a tiding arrives, unobstructed by any of the doors, which are always left open. The new tiding is then whispered from one person to a second (2043–48) and wonderfully starts to grow (2059)—to "eche," 'increase'. And as the tiding is passed on there is "evermor . . . more encres" (2074–75). "Wente every tydyng fro mouth to mouth, / And that encresing ever moo. . ." (2076–77).

> And whan that was ful yspronge,
> And woxen more on every tonge
> Than ever hit was, hit wente anoon
> Up to a wyndowe out to goon. (2081–84)

So far we have only how a rumor takes on a life of its own. Once the tiding gets out the window, however, it goes straight to Fame, "And she yeven ech hys name" (2112).[22] Now the fragile wicker house that the tiding has just left is preserved by Fame's sister Chance, or Fortune, whom Chaucer calls "the moder" of tidings (1982–83).[23] On the one hand, then, the feminine is altogether erased from this hollow, whirling cage. On the other, in the unconscious of the text, the cage itself by an ellipsis becomes the "moder" that preserves it—becomes, that is, the "moder of tydynges," which are incubated within it until they grow to

the point where they must get out, and immediately get a name. It is not
that tidings are somehow an allegory for children, which have otherwise vanished from the poem. Rather, in taking up a particular cultural
product (namely, the "milia rumorum" of a specific literary tradition),
the poet writes of the tiding as if it were also a biological product,
growing within a mother until it becomes present before a name-giver.

Consequently, when we return to Fame in the company of these
newly emerged tidings, we approach, in some sense, the father. The
poem has insisted that Fame is "a femynyne creature" (1365). Moreover, in the inconstancy of her treatment of the nine companies of ap-
plicants, she resembles Lady Meed in *Piers Plowman,* who, "fikel of
hire speche," "maketh men mysdo many score tymes" (B.3.122–23).
In other words, as Clare Lees writes of Meed elsewhere in this volume,
Fame acts "just like a woman." Having said this, however, we are also
aware that giving fame means giving a name. Literally, this means 'reputation.' Figuratively, it is a proper name itself. The word "fame" appears as an end-rhyme in twenty-two couplets throughout the poem.
While "name" is hardly the only word that could rhyme with it, the
two in fact make up the rhyme on sixteen of the twenty-two occasions.
And on all but three, "name" has the sense of one's proper name.[24] For
example, the narrator sees how the northern slope of the hill of ice
"was writen ful of names / Of folkes that hadden grete fames . . ."
(1153–54). Thus, Fame becomes linked in the unconscious of the text
with the proper name. The heralds and pursuivants blessing those who
"wilnen to have name" are bringing coats of arms (1312–40).

In fourteenth-century England, the father indelibly gave a name to
the child, not in the sense that surviving records can tell us who controlled the choice of godfather or godmother and therefore the choice of
the baptismal name, but in the sense that by the middle of the fourteenth century in England it was common practice for the child to take
the surname of a parent. While this might be the mother's when the
mother was chief inheritor of her family's land (Hanawalt, 175), that
was only rarely the case, as a line added to the C text of *Piers Plowman*
suggests: "And that is nat reasonable ne rect to refuse my syre name,
/ Sethe y am his sone and his seruant and his seruant sewe for his
ryhte."[25] The line in *Piers* resonates with the question Fame asks a
group who want to be left to hide their good works in obscurity:
"What?" she says, "Have ye dispit to have my name?" (1716). As
Shulamith Shahar has reported, didactic authors commonly took the

view that children, by bearing their father's name, perpetuated his memory and that of his forefathers.[26]

Since the rise of feudal institutions, the control of reproduction signified by the imposition of a name is massively accomplished by the substitution of agnate for cognate inheritance. The practice from about 1300 of entailing estates usually meant that a rule of primogeniture would be applied through subsequent generations.[27] In peasant families as in aristocratic, women were evidently not, as Barbara Hanawalt has remarked, "part of their family's strategy for economic and social success. . . ."[28] Consequently, the economic and political dependency of children upon the father necessarily meant that, within limits, women were situated in such dependency as well. Typically women did not inherit land, and they could not make wills leaving it to someone else. Already in the late tenth and eleventh centuries, the practice of bridegift, often land that the woman "owned outright and could alienate or leave to whomever she wished," was being replaced by the dower, which gave the woman the use during her lifetime of a portion, "usually one-third," of her husband's patrimony. "She was thus provided for in case of her husband's decease but her economic independence during his lifetime, and, to some extent, after his death, had vanished."[29] In a society in which nine-tenths of all wealth rested upon agriculture and in which the political sphere had not yet been separated from the economic, the economic disabling of the woman that is both reflected and partially accomplished by imposition of the paternal name is inseparable from political disabilities.[30]

Chaucer has divided the Ovidian house of Fame to put Fame in the position of the name-giver to the newly emerged, like the father within real houses. The poem ends with the converse of this. "A man of gret auctorite" creates a stir by turning up in the place of the "moder" (2158). When the poem thus turns itself inside out, it may well reach an impasse: men of "gret auctorite" are what the poem would sustain, and they cannot be made absurd. Yet one of them, able by definition to write the child into the order of words, absurdly appears in the whirling womb and is assimilated to the unnamed: "y saugh a man, / Which that y nevene nat ne kan" (2155–60).

Chaucer modifies Ovid by spinning off a scene of gestation after he has specified *Fama* as the imposition of a name. The woman having thus become the name-giver, Chaucer composes her femininity precisely as an incompetence. In giving a name, the father calls the child to take a particular place within social relations, at a time when the surname itself was a social endowment, defining the father as Smith or Weaver. With the name comes, in principle, the Law. But Fame is precisely useless for this purpose: she boasts there is in her "no justice" (1820). The way she proceeds—for instance, arbitrarily creating or destroying the reputation of identical groups of virtuous men—leaves the narrator dumbfounded: "With that aboute y clew myn hed" (1702). This presumably models the reader's own consternated amusement, for Chaucer has conflated the behavior of Fortune and Fame, disturbing what Laura Kendrick has called "the fundamental premise of chivalric ideology": "fame is not arbitrary."[31] The poem insists on the labor of giving people the glory they deserve. The writers of "olde gestes" (1515), from Fame herself, so far as she upholds Alexander and Hercules, to Claudius's account of Pluto and Persephone, tell the truth. (If Homer lied [1477–80], even the envious blame him only for partiality to the "Grekes," not willful randomness.) But this usual reliability is simply the background for Fame's antic moment, which functions to leave fathers in place.

A text in which Fame, a woman, usurps the father's place and makes a shambles of it reinforces the position of the father within patriarchal society. His position is reinforced also so far as he is shown to be critically important to the welfare of the child. It is reinforced even when the power is punitive, as in Jupiter's substituting himself for Apollo in acting against Phaethon (955–56).[32] Venus, who cannot protect them herself, must implore Jupiter to protect the ships of "hir sone," Aeneas (215–18). And although the narrator describes himself as an attentive servant to Cupid "and faire Venus also" (617–18), Jupiter, not Venus, arranges "som recompensacion" for him (665), dispatching the eagle, who, swearing by "Seynte Marye" (573) and carrying a living burden under his belly, supplements and displaces the maternal labor. Among the entertainers in Fame's house are "Phitonesses, charmeresses," accompanied by "Old wicches, sorceresses, / That used exorsisacions, / And eke these fumygacions" (1261–64). No doubt they represent the apparitiousness, the unreliability, that Chaucer means to contrast with writing. Yet they inscribe as well a fear contemporary with Chaucer "that witches were interfering with the natural fertility crucial to an agrarian society." "It is as if," Kathleen Casey goes on to say, these contemporaries "clearly saw how dangerous it would be for women to take control over reproduction."[33] Because everything getting its name in Chaucer's "hous" *comes from somewhere else*, this danger, within the project of the text, cannot emerge. Unpredictability may be gendered "femynyne" in the poem, but treachery is reserved for the male.

The same whirling house that acts on an imperative within the ideology of gender enters the opposition of class. Apart from the reductive reference to "Jakke Straw and his meynee" in the Nun's Priest's Tale (7.3394), Chaucer does not let on that people are divided by class interests. In the *Hous of Fame* the fact of exploitation is displaced to Aeolus's keeping the winds in severe bondage (1586–90); and the fact of resistance—the revolt of 1381, for instance—is displaced into stones hurled from a siege machine that is only metaphoric (1934), a figure for the air rushing through the twigs as the second house revolves as swiftly as thought (1924). That the *Hous* takes a side in class conflict becomes visible yet again only through disjunctions and contradictions within the text.

Chaucer divides Ovid's house along glaring class lines. The house of twigs (1936, 1941), sixty miles in length (1979), stands in a valley below the castle (1917–20). The peasant life called up by the "hottes," "panyers," and "dossers" to which the house is likened is represented also by Chaucer's homely figure for the circulation of news: all the sheaves get out of the barn sooner or later (2139–40). Peasant life is suggested too by Chaucer's metaphor for noise off in one corner: men "troden fast on others heles, / And stampen, as men doon aftir eles" (2153–54). Those who bring the news in this house are the pardoners, shipmen, and pilgrims who might turn up in seaside or inland hamlets. They are not the heralds and harpers populating the castle. As Stephen Knight has pointed out, the wicker house is a peasant house.[34] When wood became scarce in the fourteenth century and generally used in peasant construction only for framing, walls between the studs consisted of wattle and daub—"a screen woven of twigs and small branches covered with mud." Archaeological study of deserted medieval villages has shown that the typical half-virgater or virgater had a long-house, normally fifty feet in length, but sometimes as long as eighty-two to ninety-eight feet, if not sixty miles (1979).

In the obvious contrast, the other half of Fame's domicile from the *Metamorphoses* comes out as an opulent castle, peopled by a military aristocracy. (This aristocracy, however, is not singled out to provide the victims of Fame's arbitrariness. The nine companies of petitioners are class-neutral, "of alleskynnes condiciouns," "pore and ryche" [1530, 1532].) This opposition between castle and long-house is static: rocks are being hurled toward the castle only figuratively. Yet there are in the poem not just the contradictions that Chaucer foregrounds—the contradictory evidence on the reliability of dreams, for instance, or the contradiction between the reputation that some petitioners have earned and the one they get. There are also the contradictions he does not foreground, those that arise from changes he makes to Ovid under the pressure of an ideological, in this case a class, imperative.

By subdividing the *domus* in Ovid, Chaucer creates a contradiction. Some critical accounts attempt to remove it: "Composed of true and false, the tidings fly from the House of Rumour to the House of Fame. Here Fame herself gives them 'name' and 'duracioun,' and Aeolus blows them about. . . ."[35] But all of heaven, earth, and sea has already been made the source of tidings for the castle (672–724). Moreover, where, in Ovid, the house has the function of reproducing and repeating what it hears ("refert iteratque quod audit" [12.47]), the eagle, prolix on the physics of sound, neglects to mention this repetition and doubling, perhaps because part of the humor of Fame's behavior will consist in her granting or denying the obscurity that some petitioners will request (1693–99, 1704–11). That is, before Fame acts, there is presumably only silence.

The most interesting contradictions from a materialist viewpoint, however, may involve Chaucer's centrifugal imagery. In explaining to Geoffrey how sounds can make their way to the house of Fame, the eagle uses an analogy from fluid of another kind, perhaps drawing on one of the widely circulated glosses on Priscian, as Martin Irvine has shown:[36]

> for yf that thow
> Throwe on water now a stoon,
> Wel wost thou hyt wol make anoon
> A litel roundell as a sercle,
> Paraunter brod as a covercle;
> And ryght anoon thow shalt see wel
> That whel wol cause another whel,
> And that the thridde, and so forth, brother,
> Every sercle causynge other
> Wydder than hymselve was;
> And thus fro roundel to compas,
> Ech aboute other goynge
> Causeth of othres sterynge
> And multiplyinge ever moo,

Til that hyt be so fer ygoo
That hyt at bothe brynkes bee. (788–803)

It is a short step from the concentric to the centrifugal: tidings must leave the whirling house like stones from a sling. Nevertheless, like other forms of air, they have a "kyndely enclynyng" (734) to Fame's house and do not need to be shot there. Fame itself, from *fari* 'to speak', "In its substaunce ys but air" (768). Like every other "lyght thing," it must naturally move "upward" (734, 746). Thus, whenever Aeolus blows a blast from either his golden or his black horn, the assertion that it becomes known anywhere else than in Fame's house (1641–42, 1724, 1770, 1807, 1867) runs counter to Chaucer's addition of the eagle's very palpable proof. The sounds approaching the castle are contradicted by the trumpet blasts that are leaving, blasts that themselves increase as they go, like the diameters of the concentric circles: the further the blast travels, "The gretter wexen hit bigan, / As dooth the ryver from a welle" (1652–53). The tidings thrown from the whirling house are likewise offset by tidings that arrive and somehow are not prevented from stepping in (1955), unlike the narrator, who cannot enter without the eagle's help, "So faste hit whirleth, lo, aboute" (2006). The house has a thousand holes so that the sound may go out (1950–51). Yet the sound also arrives unobstructed: no porter prevents "No maner tydynges in to pace" (1955).

These contradictions between forces coincide with the contradiction that the "tydynges" within the wicker house are not simply events but already the reports of these, "rounynges" and "jangles / Of werres, of pes," and so on (1960). Creatures there already whisper what someone has "sayd" or what "he doth" (2052). Although the reader has understood that "werkes" must go to Fame's house to have a "name" (1558, 1556), they in fact have already been named and renamed (2059–62). This disjunction in the text coincides with a contradiction in the castle that I have already mentioned. The eagle accounts for the arrival of speech. Yet there is no speech—at any rate, no speech that praises or blames—until Aeolus blows his horn. This contradiction is captured by two of the questions put to Geoffrey in the castle by an unnamed person: (1) whether Geoffrey has come to have fame (1872) and (2) what are the tidings that Geoffrey has brought (1907–909).[37]

These glaring yet unspoken contradictions express and suppress a contradiction within feudalism itself. The contradiction consists in the

fact that, within feudal relations of production, the land is, by custom
and enforceable right, occupied by the direct producer, whether free or
servile. Because titles to peasant holdings were protected by manorial
custom, it was the case that "in different contexts the question, 'Whose
land is this?,' would be answered, equally correctly, by giving the name
of the lord, the peasant, or possibly that of some intermediate
tenant."[38] In the *Grundrisse,* Marx identifies as an element in feudal
relations the "appropriation of the natural conditions of labour, of the
earth as the original instrument of labour"—"appropriation not by
means of labour, but as the preliminary condition of labour. The individual simply regards the objective conditions of labour as his
own. . . ."[39] Because the land was thus in the hands of the peasant to
begin with, productive relations within feudalism are defined by the
lord's need for political means if he is to protect a surplus in the peasant's labors and extract some or all of it. Feudal relations of production
are therefore defined by the economic never emerging as such, but re-
maining indissoluble from a political relation—specifically, the political ascendancy of the aristocracy. The feudal relations of production
presuppose this ascendancy. "How does the landlord prevent the appropriation of the land by the direct producers? . . . To exact rent supposes not only a general title to property enforced by the state, but the
political dominance of the landlord class."[40]

Thus, an "inbuilt contradiction," in Perry Anderson's phrase, tor-
ments feudalism, a contradiction "between its own rigorous tendency
to a decomposition of sovereignty and the absolute exigences of a final
center of authority in which a practical recomposition could occur."[41]
This contradiction between a tendency to a decomposition on the one
hand and, on the other, the absolute exigencies of a final center is both
expressed and suppressed in the *Hous of Fame.* This contradiction is
*ex*pressed so far as class locations are made explicit, although they are
turned at once into sending and receiving stations, where communica-
tion takes place because of physical, not political or economic forces.
The contradiction is *ex*pressed so far as the poem assigns offsetting
forces to each and foregrounds them as always centrifugal. Any two
centers of force oppose each other without resolution. But the contradiction is *sup*pressed so far as a contradiction bedeviling the ruling
class is mystified as a contradiction proper to the castle and the long-
house alike.

The silent historical conflicts in the poem are reflected in its own
contradictions, which it would contain within comic limits or silently

naturalize as occurring everywhere. If they occur everywhere, then the poem would have us believe that they occur outside any particular conflict. That they do not becomes evident in the incommensurability—yet another contradiction—between Chaucer's Ovidian source and the imperatives of both gender and class on which he acts.

Gender and class, then, unite for him in an ideological project coordinating a class interest with a gender one. Castle and long-house cooperate in renewing the feminine dependency on which the beginning of the poem insisted. But this cooperation is signified by a cooperation in which the long-house delivers its products to the castle without complaint, as if rents and feudal fines are being cheerfully paid. The object of gender struggle and the object of class struggle are thus condensed into one. That such a condensation can occur is an index to the difference between cultural production considered as ideological and as economic. Where gender and class are irreducible at the economic level, the tropes of the poem, because metaphoricity is already a matter of multiple signification, disguise their reproductive force within history precisely by acting within both contests simultaneously.[42]

Notes

1. See Annette Kuhn and AnnMarie Wolpe, "Feminism and Materialism," in *Feminism and Materialism: Women and Modes of Production*, ed. Kuhn and Wolpe (London: Routledge and Kegan Paul, 1978), 8. While Marxist analysis has generally given scant attention to the oppression of women, it may also be true that "an exclusive focus on male/female conflict serves as a distraction from other kinds of conflict": Mary Childers and bell hooks, "A Conversation about Race and Class," in *Conflicts in Feminism*, ed. Marianne Hirsch and Evelyn Fox Keller (New York: Routledge, 1990), 63. For example, Gayatri Spivak has recently shown how "the emergent perspective of feminist criticism reproduces the axioms of imperialism. A basically isolationist admiration for the literature of the female subject in Europe and Anglo-America establishes the high feminist norm": "Three Women's Texts and a Critique of Imperialism," *Critical Inquiry* 12 (1985): 243.

2. See Kaplan, *Sea Changes: Essays on Culture and Feminism* (London: Verso, 1986), 165.

3. To attempt to theorize the relations between class and gender struggle is not to suggest a "theory of woman" herself. For the difficulty of theorizing the feminine (but also, conversely, of declining to theorize it) see Jane Gallop, *The*

Daughter's Seduction: Feminism and Psychoanalysis (Ithaca: Cornell University Press, 1982), 63. Annette Kolodny is perhaps the best known proponent of the view that the analysis of gender analysis can make do with already established methods of literary criticism. See, for example, her "Turning the Lens on 'The Panther Captivity': A Feminist Exercise in Practical Criticism," *Critical Inquiry* 8 (1981): 345.

4. Hartmann, "The Unhappy Marriage of Marxism and Feminism: Towards a More Progressive Union," in *Women and Revolution*, ed. Lydia Sargent (Boston: South End, 1981), 9–10 (her emphasis). One appropriation of Marxist methodology for feminist analysis is the Marxist-Feminist Literature Collective's use of "the ideas of Jacques Lacan, Pierre Macherey, and others" to recover portions of women's history. For example, through a "symptomatic" reading, the Collective recovers "woman as a desiring subject," "the urgent plight of dependent women" as the "not-said" of certain texts. See "Women's Writing: *Jane Eyre, Shirley, Villette,* and *Aurora Leigh," Ideology and Consciousness* 3 (Spring 1978): 27–48. In this chapter, I follow Hartmann in a "dual systems" approach. One problem with a "single-system" theory like Iris Young's, in which "the oppression of women is a *core* attribute" of "capitalist patriarchy," is that the history of patriarchy becomes subordinated to the history of the social relations of production: that is, the history of the oppression of women is made inextricable from the development from feudalism to capitalism. See Young, "Beyond the Unhapppy Marriage: A Critique of the Dual Systems Theory," in *Women and Revolution*, 44. Young uses the "gender division of labor" to explain this single system (e.g., p. 55). But it is the "gender division of labor," I think, that needs to be theorized. See, for example, Stephanie Coontz and Peta Henderson, *Women's Work, Men's Property* (London: Verso, 1986).

5. Thus there is nothing in Marxist analysis that necessarily naturalizes gender—for example, through a natural division of labor in the family. But see Monique Wittig, "The Category of Sex," *Feminist Issues* 2 (1982): 66.

6. Karl Marx and Frederick Engels, *The German Ideology* (Moscow: Progress, 1964), 85.

7. Frederick Engels, *The Origin of the Family, Private Property, and the State* (New York: International, 1942), 71.

8. *Chaucer Life-Records,* ed. Martin M. Crow and Clair C. Olson (Oxford: Clarendon, 1966), 3.

9. Barrett, *Women's Oppression Today: The Marxist/Feminist Encounter,* rev. ed. (London: Verso, 1988), 226. With the reallocation of childcare, the father becomes a second pre-Oedipal object for both little boys and little girls. The gender roles that are offered in the Oedipal period would thus interpellate subjects whose sexual histories would be different than they are now, when childcare falls largely upon mothers. In this way, one outcome of gender struggle would affect the psychological terrain on which further gender struggle would be played out. (For example, infantile anger arising because of the child's inevitable disappointments would be distributed more evenly between mother and father.) Moreover, the gender roles themselves offered in the Oedipal period would change, because the father's work would no longer be entirely distant and abstract, by contrast with the mother's; and finally, the depth

of identifications by children of either gender would change because of that. In short, the genders that arise in struggle change with the struggle. Gender roles function at the political "instance" within gender contest to reproduce the genders, but their nature is determined by the course of the contest itself. For one study of the consequences of women's mothering, see Nancy J. Chodorow, *Feminism and Psychoanalytic Theory* (New Haven: Yale University Press, 1989).

10. See Louis Althusser, "Ideology and Ideological State Apparatuses (Notes Towards an Investigation)," in *"Lenin and Philosophy" and Other Essays*, trans. Ben Brewster (New York: Monthly Review, 1971), 134. For one of many critiques of Althusser, see Ernesto Laclau and Chantal Mouffe, *Hegemony and Socialist Strategy*, trans. Winston Moore and Paul Cammack (London: Verso, 1985), 97–105. For a recent defense, see Michael Sprinker, *Imaginary Relations: Aesthetics and Ideology in the Theory of Historical Materialism* (London: Verso, 1987), 192–205. "The concept of 'relative autonomy,' " Michèle Barrett has written, "must, whatever its apparent fragility, be further explored and defined. . . . What [this further exploration would involve] is the specification, for a given social historical context, of the limits to the autonomous operation of ideology. Hence we should be able to specify what range of possibilities exist for the ideological processes of a particular social formation, without necessarily being able to predict the specific form they may take": "Ideology and the Cultural Production of Gender," in *Feminist Criticism and Social Change*, ed. Judith Newton and Deborah Rosenfelt (New York: Methuen, 1985), 73.

11. David Herlihy, *Medieval Households* (Cambridge, MA: Harvard University Press, 1985), 97.

12. See Eleanor Searle, *Lordship and Community: Battle Abbey and Its Banlieu, 1066–1538* (Toronto: Pontifical Institute, 1974), 415, 407, 390 (her emphasis).

13. See Herlihy, 81–82. Coroners' inquests into the cause of peasant women's death confirm that their work sphere was the home, just as men's was the field and forests: see Barbara Hanawalt, "Peasant Women's Contribution to the Home Economy in Late Medieval England," in *Women and Work in Pre-Industrial Europe*, ed. Hanawalt (Bloomington: Indiana University Press, 1986), 7.

14. Chris Middleton, "Women's Labour and the Transition to Pre-Industrial Capitalism," in *Women and Work in Pre-Industrial England*, ed. Lindsey Charles and Lorna Duffin (London: Croom Helm, 1985), 197. Hartmann gives a modern example of such coordinated activity within the analytically distinguishable struggles of class and gender. When English and American capitalists supported the "family wage" in the nineteenth century, they encouraged women "to choose wifery as a career," with men as the material beneficiaries. But the "family wage" thus divided the working force and increased the pool of reserve labor. See "The Unhappy Marriage," 22.

15. A materialist criticism, therefore, is clearly incomplete in principle until it takes into account not only the distinguishable contests of class and gender but potentially others as well—race, for instance, once a material basis for it has been adequately theorized.

16. See Macherey, *A Theory of Literary Production,* trans. Geoffrey Wall (London: Routledge and Kegan Paul, 1978), esp. 91–93.

17. Chaucer will be cited throughout from *The Riverside Chaucer,* 3rd ed. ed. Larry D. Benson et al. (Boston: Houghton Mifflin, 1987).

18. *Chaucer's* Book of Fame (Oxford: Clarendon, 1968), 174.

19. Ovid, *Metamorphoses,* ed. and trans. F. J. Miller, 3rd ed. (Cambridge: Harvard University Press, 1977).

20. This has recently been emphasized by Edward Vasta, "Narrative Pessimism and Textual Optimism in Chaucer's *House of Fame,*" in *The Work of Dissimilitude: Essays from the Sixth Citadel Conference on Medieval and Renaissance Literature,* ed. D. G. Allen and R. A. White (Newark: University of Delaware Press; London: Associated University Presses, 1992), 35–47.

21. *Chaucer and the Fictions of Gender* (Berkeley: University of California Press, 1992), 96–97.

22. In the house of *Fama* in Ovid, there are no doors that might close up openings (12.45); in Chaucer, there are doors, but all are left open (1952–53). It is just possible that Chaucer adds the doors but does not lock them because, at some level, he knows of the tradition in which midwives, by way of sympathetic magic, leave chests and doors unlocked as a removal of impediments to childbirth. See Angus McLaren, *Reproductive Rituals: The Perception of Fertility in England from the Sixteenth Century to the Nineteenth Century* (London: Methuen, 1984), 51. I owe this reference to my colleague, Frances Dolan.

23. Piero Boitani describes Chance as "a power even more arbitrary than Fortune," but, in the *Hous of Fame* at least, this seems to me a distinction without a difference. See *Chaucer and the Imaginary World of Fame* (Cambridge, England: Brewer, 1984), 174.

24. See lines 306, 1145, 1275, 1405, 1411, 1462, 1489, 1556, 1610, 1696, 1716, 1736, and 1871.

25. Piers Plowman: *An Edition of the C-Text,* ed. Derek Pearsall (Berkeley: University of California Press, 1979), 3.366–7.

26. *The Fourth Estate: A History of Women in the Middle Ages,* ed. Chaya Galai (London: Methuen, 1983), 99. Cf. Herlihy, 97.

27. See Herlihy, 93–94.

28. "Peasant Women's Contribution," 6. Cf. Herlihy, 137. There were clearly exceptions. On the manors of Battle Abbey, "female partible inheritance was a not inconsiderable factor in splitting the original tenements" (Searle, 119).

29. Jo Ann McNamara and Suzanne Wemple, "The Power of Women through the Family in Medieval Europe, 500–1100," in *Women and Power in the Middle Ages,* ed. Maryanne Kowaleski and Mary Erler (Athens: University of Georgia Press, 1988), 96.

30. Writing of village women in Brigstock, Judith M. Bennett concludes that all of them "faced political, economic, legal, and social disadvantages unknown to men. . .": *Women in the Medieval English Countryside: Gender and Household in Brigstock before the Plague* (New York: Oxford University Press, 1987), 178. Cf. Lacey, 32–40. On the disabilities of townswomen, see Shahar, 197. It is reasonable to suspect that the political disability issuing from agnatic inheritance and the dynastic lineage accounts for male ability to place

renewed importance upon the dowry and to shift "the chief 'burdens of matrimony' once again on the bride and her family"—a change clearest in Italy. See Herlihy, 98.

31. See "Fame's Fabrication," *Studies in the Age of Chaucer: Proceedings* 1 (1984): 136.

32. After Geoffrey has swooned, the eagle says to him "in mannes vois," "Awak!" (556). This is "the same vois and stevene" of someone that the narrator "koude nevene" if he wished to, who nevertheless did not habitually speak to him so "goodly" as the eagle did (562, 565–66). Where the *Riverside Chaucer* follows Skeat and J. A. W. Bennett respectively in proposing that "The familiar *vois* and *stevene*" belong either to Chaucer's wife or servant, I suggest he remembered from childhood the "mannes vois" of his father.

33. Kathleen Casey, "The Cheshire Cat: Reconstructing the Experience of Medieval Women," in *Liberating Women's History*, ed. B. A. Carroll (Urbana: University of Chicago Press, 1976), 241. A trace of suspicion appears in Chaucer's description of the muses, who "in her face *semen* meke" (1402; my emphasis).

34. See *Geoffrey Chaucer* (Oxford: Blackwell, 1986), 4. Cf. J. A. W. Bennett, 169, and Barbara A. Hanawalt, *The Ties That Bound: Peasant Families in Medieval England* (New York: Oxford University Press, 1986), 34.

35. Boitani, 211. Cf. Sheila Delany, *Chaucer's* House of Fame: *The Poetics of Skeptical Fideism* (Chicago: University of Chicago Press, 1972), 105–12. It is not clear that, as Delany proposes, the petitioners in the castle "have been resurrected" (105). For example, the sixth company wishes to be perceived as if "wommen loven [them] for wod" (1747)—something that would be going on presently. Delany understands Fame to differ from Rumour as finished history differs from history in the making. Her study, of course, points to another kind of insoluble "inner contradiction" within the poem (109).

36. "Medieval Grammatical Theory and Chaucer's *House of Fame*," *Speculum* 60 (1985): 865.

37. This episode has recently been discussed by J. Stephen Russell, "A Seme in the Integument: Allegory in the *Hous of Fame*," in *Allegoresis: The Craft of Allegory in Medieval Literature*, ed. Russell (New York: Garland, 1988), 171–85.

38. J. A. F. Thomson, *The Transformation of Medieval England, 1370–1529* (London: Longman, 1983), 18.

39. Karl Marx, *Pre-Capitalist Economic Formations*, trans. Jack Cohen, ed. E. J. Hobsbawm (New York: International, 1964), 81.

40. Barry Hindess and Paul Q. Hirst, *Pre-Capitalist Modes of Production* (London: Routledge, 1975), 241.

41. *Passages from Antiquity to Feudalism* (London: NLB, 1974), 152.

42. I thank Frances Dolan for her helpful reading of this essay.

Gender and Exchange in
Piers Plowman

* * *

Clare A. Lees

> Like the value of a commodity, women's sexual de-
> sirability is fetishized: it is made to appear a quality
> of the object itself, spontaneous and inherent, inde-
> pendent of the social relation which creates it, un-
> controlled by the force that requires it.

Catharine A. MacKinnon[1]

The project of these chapters, which explore the linking of class analysis with gender analysis in medieval literature, is based on one other
self-evident intersection, namely that medievalists share a common interest in trying to understand the material nature of the past—its social
formations, beliefs, and cultural practices—whatever the methodolo-
gies we use. The different emphases, both theoretical and practical, of
gender studies and class analysis, however, can sometimes seem to
sever this intersection. Much feminist medieval scholarship rightly con-
centrates on examining the representation of *women* in society and culture and on recovering their history and agency—priorities that
occasionally obscure how women are implicated in the classes or ranks
of medieval social hierarchies. Materialist criticism, on the other hand,
tends to lay out the broader issues of the relations of production of
wealth; here class analysis is directly implicated, although the terms by
which class is defined, at least traditionally, can subsume the vexed issue of women's work.[2] These different emphases are best viewed as
implicitly related and complementary, even (or especially) when there
remains a fundamental but, I would argue, healthy political skepticism
about how much a feminist agenda is enhanced by materialist theories,
and vice versa.[3]

Rather than dwell on our differences, then, I want to outline some of
the common ground that strengthens, for me at least, the argument for

sustaining a dialogue between gender and class analysis in medieval literature. First, the concept of the household, and the organization of labor within it, has become increasingly targeted as an important site for understanding the relations of production in feudalism; second, the family is necessarily the main unit of reproduction, both of itself and of the production of the labor force; third, since the family so produced can be both patriarchal and patrilineal, the family (like the household) generates gender asymmetries, which are complemented by the evident gender asymmetries of medieval institutions—the law, the Church, and so on.[4] Buttressed by religious and secular ideologies, the concept of the family is fundamental to the institutionalization of heterosexual desire, whereby woman-as-object-of-desire is replaced by woman-as-wife-and-mother. In addition, the reproduction of the family maintains, at least in part, the reproduction of class difference, from which the aristocrat no less than the merchant or peasant derives social identity. In the theoretical construct of "family," in other words, desire, production, and reproduction are all interrelated.

The concepts of labor, household, and the family are not only integral to one another, they are also potential sites of conflict because feudalism is based on unequal distribution of power, across the sexes as much as across the classes.[5] It is hardly surprising, then, that medievalists have recently begun to explore the nature and forces of production and/or desire as we test our own theories of feudalism against the material record. These two issues of production and desire are, of course, simply manifestations of an intersection between class and gender. By concentrating on the social construction of gender, for example, feminist work brings to light some of the conflicts inherent in medieval society—as much by examining medieval women's work as by considering the representation of gender asymmetries and the workings of desire in medieval texts.[6] It is precisely these kinds of conflicts that the ideology of the three estates seeks to naturalize and thereby mystify (there are no women among the rulers, the ruled, and the worshipers), and that medieval texts, almost in spite of themselves, can barely conceal.

I dismiss pragmatically, therefore, the many theoretical objections to what is often more generally (and sometimes misleadingly) known as the "unhappy marriage"[7] of materialism and feminism, and concentrate instead on examining another unconsummated marriage, that of Mede in *Piers Plowman*, from a position that embraces both perspectives.[8] For the purposes of this experimental reading, I focus mainly on the representation of Mede and engage more directly with issues of gender than those of class. In the process of reading Mede (herself an aristocratic figure), however, I shall demonstrate how Langland explores the two issues of production and desire that I have already suggested are central to our understanding of feudalism.

My choice of text is no accident. *Piers Plowman*—long a favorite of medievalists interested in the relationship between literature and history—has more recently become the focus of materialist readings, most notably and most rigorously by David Aers and Britton J. Harwood, but the poem has attracted few critics interested in gender.[9] I am drawn to the figure of Mede in Passus II–IV of *Piers* (chiefly the B text) for several reasons. What engages my attention is the way that the complex of issues explored in the Prologue and early passus of the poem—the descriptions of the use and circulation of wealth, value, reward, and desire in the social world that is the "fair field" of the Prologue—are channeled into the personified figure of Mede as a woman and expressed through a narrative of the legal institution of marriage. Most scholarship on this issue has quite naturally concentrated on defining Mede: much of the poem is, of course, preoccupied with the same question. In fact, the range of critical interpretations is initially bewildering: Mede is, for example, a type of the Whore of Babylon, the antithesis of Holy Church, a counterpart to Richesse in the *Roman de la Rose;* a barely concealed representation of Alice Perrers, mistress to Edward III; an aristocratic ward and relation to the king used to test the viability of his prerogative courts; an apt encoding of *pecunia* as *cupiditas,* and so forth.[10]

Whatever Mede *is* (and clearly she is many things), Langland's personification generates a powerful desire to fix her, to close her. Or, to put it another way, the question of why Mede is female, a question of gender, is subordinated to the meaning of the allegory that is her story, even by those critics who do take Mede's sex into account. I want to demonstrate this point by considering briefly several critical approaches to Mede.

Perhaps the most obvious case (though an unexplored one) for Mede's gender as a textual figure is her scriptural type—as the antithesis of Holy Church; it is theologically appropriate that she is reminiscent of the Whore of Babylon (Apocalypsis 17, 5–4). Exegesis thus refers Mede to Scripture, finds confirmation of her gender in typology, and fails to ask the question: why female? This is the predominant method by which critics arrive at the meaning of Mede; one that is commonly brought to bear on allegory in general, and on personification allegory in specific. The letter of Mede is translated into, or replaced by, something else, something other.[11] The greatest insight of scholarship on Langland's Mede, however, is that she always means at least two things (woman and money to state only the most obvious) in relation to a third term, the word itself, "mede." Mede's literary genealogy, for example, is drawn largely from the world of medieval venality satire, as John A. Yunck's important study reminds us. In this genre, personifications of wealth are most often female: the genre confirms the sex of the figure in Langland's poem and the question of Mede's gender again remains unasked. Unless we consider this question, however, we are in danger of overlooking the simple point that Mede is not necessarily or even exclusively a female figure in the genre of venality satire.[12] Since Mede can be textually masculine in this genre, Langland's choice of gender may be highly significant.

Arguing that she approaches the question of Mede from the historical perspective of the fourteenth century, Anna P. Baldwin draws attention to Mede's gender by noting that, as a woman and relative of the king, she is necessarily under his protection and part of his interest.[13] Her trial, therefore, is used by Langland to examine the theory and practices of the king's prerogative courts. The greatest threat to the king's power is presented as female, the vehicle of the threat is a marriage, and the locus is the prerogative court, as Baldwin astutely points out. But the gender of Mede is of more significance than Baldwin suggests precisely because as "woman" (and not simply a literary version of Alice Perrers), Mede would have little power to represent her legal interests. As is well known, medieval women were severely disadvantaged before the law, where they were barred from key positions and had much less ability to influence decisions than Langland suggests.[14] As a woman, Mede's ability to corrupt the law by giving bribes would be much more compromised than any man's, and Langland's narrative obscures the fact that men have far more power to participate in and to influence legal decisions than women. That Baldwin does not address this as she translates the allegory of Mede into "history" indicates how little she has considered the equally historical issue of gender as a social system of female oppression.

But it is one other set of readings that most clearly demonstrates how the question of Mede's gender remains subordinate to the question of her allegory. Critics such as C. David Benson, Malcolm Godden, and A. G. Mitchell deal with Mede's gender by praising the aptness of

Langland's figurative construction without considering its implications.[15] By a neat sleight of hand, the problem of the personification of
Mede as female is displaced onto a demonstration of the appropriate-
ness of the personification to the letter. Godden offers a useful summary of this critical position:

> The fundamental question about the place of wealth in the good society
> is brilliantly captured in the ambivalence of Mede's own personality:
> beautiful innocent led astray by those around her, or magnetic courtesan
> cynically corrupting all she can reach?[16]

There is little remarkable here. Godden simply restates a well-known
position on Mede, namely that the ambivalence of her figure expresses
Langland's ambivalence toward the uses and abuses of reward in these
passus of the poem. But, as a textual figure, Mede is ambiguous rather
than ambivalent. What Godden actually captures is the ambivalence
that most figures in the poem, and most critics as well, express toward
her: *potentially both wife and whore, Mede clearly behaves just like a
woman.* There are thus two medes (the reward and the bribe) and two
women (the wife and the whore) all represented by the same figure: the
ambiguous, immoral, ambivalent mede who refuses no man. Furthermore, if Mede is a "magnetic courtesan," as Godden suggests, then
she is that mythical whore with the heart of gold. No one pays Mede for
services rendered, though she is generous with her services. Mede becomes neither wife nor prostitute and, indeed, is emotionally distressed
to discover herself labeled a whore—a term that addresses more her
apparent sexual promiscuity than her role as a prostitute—when she is
summarily dismissed in Passus IV: "Mede mornede þo and made heuy
chere, / For þe mooste commune of þat court called hire an hore" (B
IV 165–66).[17] Nor is Mede anywhere described as a "beautiful innocent," to return to Godden. But my general point is clear: Mede's representation as a textual figure is overdetermined by issues of gender,
expressed in binary terms as the potential wife or the seductive whore.
These symptoms of overdetermination, moreover, are both internal and
external to the poem, as Godden's exaggerated reading of Mede as in-
nocent/courtesan indicates.[18] Grouping together the interpretations of
Yunck, Baldwin, and Godden, we glimpse the powerful hold on the
critical imagination exerted by the construct: women/money.

Mede's gender thus emerges as the unanalyzed ground of, and key
to, her textual representation and critical interpretation. Why Mede is

felt to be so female or why her femaleness is an adequate expression of material wealth, or indeed why the allegory concerns marriage remains to be addressed.

In order to focus more closely on Mede's gender, I want to reexamine the literal letter of the allegory—the level most usually overlooked in critical analysis. Instead of looking at *who* she is in order to discover what she means, I suggest we examine *how* she is. Or rather, how Mede is produced as female by the processes of use and exchange that mark Passus II–IV of the poem. The immediate advantage of such an approach is that it addresses not beginnings and ends but the processes which create them. Such a reading enables us to recover Mede's position in her narrative as that of produced object, even when she is the ostensible subject. As object, she functions in two interrelated ways: as wealth and as woman. Marx points out that objects or "commodities" have a utility, a use-value, that is strictly limited to the properties of the thing, but that:

> Use-values become a reality only by use or consumption: they also constitute the substance of all wealth, whatever may be the social form of that wealth . . . they are, in addition, the material depositories of exchange value.[19]

Indeed, the meaning of Mede is inescapably associated with how men exchange her, with masculine desires for woman and wealth. Passus II–IV are preoccupied with examining how Mede circulates in society because only the exchanged object is the "material depository" of value, whether it be Mede's value as a woman or as a reward/bribe.

It is here that I see the possibility of linking material and gender analyses with a more conventional reading of the poem. Langland chooses to explore the question of Mede, which concerns the ethical status of the desire for reward in society, with recourse to a standard literary figure inherited from the genre of venality satire. What he does, in effect, is displace the newly pressing issue of the social circulation of money onto the issue of the more traditional institutions of the patrilinear family and patriarchal marriage. The narrative of Mede's marriage enacts the process of men's desire for her: who wants her and who wants to marry her. Mede is therefore rightly the object—not the subject—of the narrative, even when she is represented as the giver, not receiver of gifts. This mystification of subject and object conceals a second mystification. As we have already seen, Langland represents Mede as simultaneously available to men as both seductive whore and potential wife. However, her representation as one single object, Mede, collapses the distinction between what is in fact two objects: first, the nature of Mede as object of men's desire; and second, the nature of Mede as exchanged object, the woman passed from man to man in marriage. *How* Mede becomes *who* she is, therefore, is predicated on her value as this double object within society: as such she represents "mede," the reward/bribe or rather the commodity, money. Desire and material value are explored through one textual figure, a woman, and any reading that separates desire from value, gender from materialism in this poem is destined to be one-sided at best.

The real question, however, involves the third mystification of Langland's narrative: how is an allegory of Mede-as-wife/whore and the trials of her marriage appropriate to an account of Mede-as-wealth (reward or bribe) and the social formations in which she circulates? What happens when men's business (to appropriate Luce Irigaray's discussion of Marx's analysis of value) is expressed as what we might call somewhat ironically "women's business"?[20] In order to understand how men's business becomes women's, we need to examine how Mede is produced as a material sign, "mede," *and* as object of desire.

A useful place to start is the dreamer's question to Holy Church at the beginning of Passus II: "Kenne me by som craft to knowe þe false" (B II 4). This does indeed produce Mede, but the description of her that follows is only indirectly the result of Holy Church's response. The dreamer/narrator alone sees and selects Mede from the group of Fals, Favel, and their companions, and the well-known description of his avid gaze dwells on her visual appearance—her furs, her jewels, her rich robes—to the extent that he declares himself "rauysshed" (B II 17) by her "array."[21] This image is laden with social significance, of course, since her dress and wealth suggest an aristocratic woman, dressed in the style of her class. What is singularly lacking in this description, however, is a female body. As a result, the dreamer is seduced by the product of his own desires, which are socially encoded. The implications of this description are profound. Mede-as-woman is fetishized by the gaze of the dreamer. In a classic act of substitution and displacement that conceals its psychogenesis, it is Mede's clothing, her "array," that is the dreamer's object of desire. At the same time, Mede-as-wealth is also presented as a fetish of the "pure commodity" of wealth, alienated from its origins in social relations, to paraphrase Marx. Langland has conflated into one overdetermined sign, "mede," two signs (women/money), which are themselves substitute signs indicated by their status as fetishes, in a brillant move only partly concealed by the direction of his narrative. These are the processes that MacKinnon identifies as analogous in the quotation that opens this chapter: "*Like* the value of a commodity, women's sexual desirability is fetishized" (my emphasis).[22]

In our initial encounter with Mede, her value expressed as her desirability is created by the dreamer/narrator's gaze, which is itself the product of a prior relationship between the dreamer and Holy Church. The process of how Mede's value can be appropriated is put into play by the dreamer's next questions: "I hadde wonder what she was and whos wif she were. / 'What is þis womman,' quod I, 'so worþili atired?'" (B II 18–19). Mede's worth, her worthy dress, is here linked to the question of ownership and expressed by the grammar of possession: "whos wif she were." In the opening lines of Passus II (5–19), Mede has been transformed, in the process of the dreamer's questioning, from object of desire into object worthy of marriage. The remainder of the marriage allegory therefore expresses the production of Mede by exploiting the connections between signs and their relations, gender and generation.

Mede's gender is, of course, in part already the product of grammatical kind, or "grammatical gender." Like its patristic gloss, *cupiditas, pecunia* is grammatically feminine, as is *ecclesia* (in the case of Holy Church). Grammatical gender, as Langland was fully aware, is one expression of the syntactic relations (via concord) that controls the production of meaning in discourse. And gender's relationship to syntax was conventionally explicated as a relationship in "kynde," in family, in medieval theories of grammar.[23]

The revisions to Conscience's discussion of the meaning of Mede in the C text make it quite clear that her multiple significations as grammatical sign, woman, and personification of reward are all interlinked, and, more importantly, that all three are necessarily interchangeable. The implicit link between these encodings in the B text ("whos wif she were") becomes explicit in the C text in Langland's use of the term "relation": "Thus is mede and mercede as two maner relacions" (C III 332). In the grammatical analogy that follows, Conscience explicates social bonds in terms of direct and indirect grammatical relations. Mede is censored as the indirect means by which *men* pursue their self-interest, which causes confusion in lineage, or name (thereby obscuring the part of Mede that is good—that is, "mercede"), as opposed to di-

rect relations where the social contract is expressed in terms of patrilineal family ties, the passing down of the family name from father to
son via marriage:

> Indirect thyng is as ho-so coueytede
> Alle kyn kynde to knowe and to folowe
> And withoute cause to cache and come to bothe nombres;
> In whiche ben gode and nat gode to graunte here neyþer will.
> And þat is nat resonable ne rect to refuse my syre name,
> Sethe y am his sone and his seruant sewe for his ryhte.
> For ho-so wolde to wyue haue my worliche douhter
> I wolde feffe hym with alle here fayre and here foule taylende.
> So indirect is inlyche to coueyte
> To acorde in alle kynde and in alle kyn nombre,
> Withouten coest and care and alle kyn trauayle.
>   (C III 362–72)[24]

It is no accident, therefore, that Conscience's analogy hinges on
grammatical gender and lineage: correct grammatical concord ensures
direct relations, direct exchange, between man and man or man and
God (C III 355–59); incorrect concord causes chaos, the indefinite,
polymorphous relations that cannot be constrained by syntax. In comparison with this excerpt in the C text, the question posed behind the
narrative of Passus II in the B text comes into plainer view: what is
Mede's *kynde* (her nature, her gender, her relation—direct or indirect)?

The B text makes the connection between linguistic signs and social
relations explicit when it discusses Mede's family. Like the sign of a
sign (or fetish) that is Mede in the dreamer's description, Mede's genealogy is the product of a prior relationship, that between her father
and her mother. This genealogy—the source of considerable anger in
Holy Church—is deliberately ambiguous and only indirectly available
to proof via Theologie's challenge. Her fathers are as interchangeable
as her intended spouses in the B text, as their names suggest: which
Fals is her father and which her intended spouse? In the A text, her
father is Wrong, and in the C text her father is Favel/Fals (an ambiguity
carried over from the B text that is never fully clarified). The conflict
over her marriage that will bring her to London is one of control over
lineage and propriety, as Holy Church's outburst makes clear. Unlike
Holy Church, who is fixed in relation to a transcendental Family—her
father is God, and she is promised to Mercy (B II 28–35)—Mede's lin-

eage has to be legally proven. The proof takes the form of two challenges: to her value, and to her line. The satiric marriage charter literalizes her worth by writing the letter of her endowments and, as a result, Holy Church's moral judgment on Mede (that she was worthy of Fals, B II 40) is reinscribed in the writ as material wealth (Falsnesse desires her because she is rich, B II 78). But Theologie, and later the king, contest control of Mede by challenging both parents (she is related to the king via her mother and therefore worthy of his interest) and partner. The family conflict is one that takes place *over* Mede in the form of a struggle over the patrilinear line—her mother, Amendes, is the link, as Theologie points out (B II 119). If Mede is married correctly, if she is given correctly (to Conscience), so the argument goes, the patrilinear line will pass via her from patriarch to patriarch: the classic definition of an aristocratic marriage.[25] In sum, it is essential to Mede's representation as exchanged object between men that the allegory takes the form of a contested marriage: she is, after all, "Mede þe mayde."

It is therefore also essential to Mede's representation that she remains potentially both direct (and thus controllable) and indirect (and thus uncontrollable); otherwise there would be no debate over her. The ambivalence that critics such as Godden register toward Mede is thus simply a result of interpreting her sign. Mede's power to generate overdetermined critical responses is itself a response to her overdetermined signification. Since Mede is always relative to the code that produces her, she cannot be fixed: as a woman she is potentially both wife and whore; as syntactical relation, she is direct and indirect; and as a daughter, she has no fixed father or spouse. Only as the product of these relations can she circulate within the economy of desire and reward in Passus II–IV. Read in this way, the marriage allegory and the trial are not simply a narrative inquiry into who Mede is, but an attempt to establish her value as exchanged object within the patriarchal systems of the family and marriage. As the discussion of her genealogy makes plain, this value depends not on any inherent quality of Mede but on the product of her relations. The point is perhaps made most effectively by the charter: "Witeþ and witnesseþ, þat wonieþ vpon erþe, / That Mede is ymaried moore *for hire goodes* / Than for any vertue or fairnesse or any free kynde" (B II 75–77).

Mede's "goodes" are her value: they are what enable her to be the focus of barter and exchange.[26] The charter initiates and witnesses her circulation as an object of value and frames her interpretation. Small wonder, then, that Mede is found in the midst of things, as is carefully pointed out, for example, in the description of her journey to London: "Fals and Fauel fareþ forþ togideres, / And Mede in þe myddes and [al þis meynee] after" (B II 184–85).

Mede is indeed always in the middle, sandwiched between Fals and Favel, Symonye and Cyuyle, Conscience and the King. Thus produced as the wife-as-exchanged object, worthy of desire for her "goodes," Mede is consumed and used up by the courts, by the economy, by marriage. She is the quiet and passive center of a veritable storm of masculine activity that passes her from father to father, spouse to spouse, the fair field to the London courts. Every man wants Mede, it would seem: some use her while some use her up.

The marriage allegory recapitulates for the dreamer the process by which Mede enters social circulation, the process whereby she is maintained in rich dress—available for men by her very absence. By the end of Passus II (B II 238–39), however, she trembles, cries, and wrings her hands: that is to say, her first response is a bodily one. In Passus III, she breaks her silence and enters the narrative, seen first dispensing gifts, or rather bribes (B III 20–91), and then responding to the King's authority over her (III 112–13) and Conscience's attack on her (III 175–229). In effect, the debate over her meaning relative to the Law in Passus II has produced the missing signifier, her body, which can only be read as a social construct. She cries and she speaks, therefore, in response to prior situations because she is already defined by the processes that make her Mede. Now that her body is reinscribed into the narrative, there is an important change in narrative direction and for good reasons since the debate has shifted from one that emphasizes her ability to be exchanged to one that stresses her desirability.

Increasingly Mede is both exchange object and object of desire collapsed into one figure: men desire her now because she gives gifts *and* because she can be used. Mede smoothes the wheels of the king's military ambitions, enhances the running of courts, facilitates trade, and cements belief, as she herself shows both by action and speech (B III 35–92; 175–227). While the passage of gifts (rewards and/or bribes) is apparently *from* Mede *to* others, the lesson of Passus II is that she cannot in fact control the direction of the gift. In a manner reminiscent of, but deliberately opposed to, the idealized mother, Holy Church, Mede now appropriates the symbolic role of mother with her acts of nurturing and of giving. She is made responsible for the success or failure of men's business as the apparent subject of Passus III but remains the object, the medium through which men conduct their affairs. What this amounts to is that Mede as medium of exchange ensures the reproduction of social institutions (trade, war, belief), just as much as she provides the potential medium through which the patrilinear family may be reproduced. At the same time, however, she also represents the uncontrollable object of men's desires and therefore cannot herself guarantee how these institutions will be reproduced. Both the king and Conscience spot the danger. But while the king seeks a temporal and temporary solution—that of control or mastery—by marrying her to Conscience, Conscience identifies and severs these central ambiguities of Mede's representation by splitting her sign semantically into "mede mesurelees" (B III 246) and "mesurable hire" (B III 256). That is to say, Conscience contrasts an immoderate desire for reward (the unsatisfiable object of desire) with a straightforward exchange object, "a penyworþ for another" (B III 258), which is further modified in the C text with the introduction of "mercede" (C III 290), a payment for services rendered. As a result of this lexical reanalysis, there is no single, unified "Mede" to marry.

In both B and C texts, however, the figure of the personified Mede still remains to be dealt with and the narrative accordingly ushers in her "fall." With the trial of Pees, Conscience adds the last phase in the restructuring of Mede's sign, transforming her back from exchanged object worthy of marriage into object of desire. Finally she is used up as Conscience puts a price on her exchange—a price that cannot pay for the worth of a man's soul, as Reason later states (B IV 134–44). Conscience denies Mede any use by limiting her value to that of the fair exchange, and by installing Reason in the court. Reason goes further because he wants to rid her from men and, moreover, wants to rid the world of the institutions that exchange her. The only logical role left for her now that she is without the variable value accumulated in exchange is that of pure use-object: Mede is thus exiled from society as the whore. In the economy of desire expressed here, the whore is a useobject *par excellence:* she possesses a marketable value as an already used commodity.[27] No one wants to marry the whore (and, in this poem at least, no one wants to pay her).

The journey traveled in the allegory is thus only superficially that from wife to whore, since Mede marries no one and her services at the end of Passus IV are little desired. Up to this point, however, Mede is defined in terms of men's desire. As product, she has no desire, no subjectivity, of her own: she represents that which is desired, not that which actively desires, and therefore she refuses no man. This is, of course, a good definition of the ideology of patriarchal marriage, an intriguing definition of the ideology of the patriarchal prostitute who seeks no reward, and, finally, a puzzling definition of Mede.

Langland performs a delicate balancing act between at least two forms of representation for Mede: the embedding of the conventional linguistic sign in a system of grammatical relations, which is in turn implicated in the embedding of the woman in a system of social relations. Both, for him, express the third term—the nature of wealth and reward as exchanged object, as sign of a sign. It is therefore absolutely essential to the allegory that Mede is personified as female, and that the story of Mede is one of marriage. In consequence, these passus suggest that aristocratic patriarchy is synonymous with the economy of the fourteenth century. The text thus pushes to the margins two rather evident problems of this intersection. First, Langland's allegory focuses on the circulation of wealth apparently within all three estates without questioning the means by which that wealth is produced.[28] No peasant, no serf, wants to marry Mede, and in fact Mede only circulates in those classes which appropriate the surplus. Second, the representation of Mede as the indirect signifier that holds together patriarchy via patrilinear relations implies at worst that women cannot own the means of production or at best that Mede, or all women, are defined by the class affiliations of their owners, or men. While this may reproduce the ideology of the three estates, it obscures the historical praxis of real women of the period, who worked, earned money and reward, and acted in their own interests as well as the interests of their classes however much they were constrained by legal definitions of their status. We need only think of the activities of London guildswomen or the rights and privileges of London widows to understand how far the ideology of the medieval estates can be from actual practice and how vexed that practice is from an interpretive standpoint.[29] In effect, the representation of Mede as both fetishized object of desire ("woman") and pure commodity ("money") conceals and displaces the social relations that produced her. It is hardly surprising, then, that Langland in his search for truth is so hostile to Mede.

Central to Langland's personification of Mede is a series of mystifications, as I have already suggested. As the single object, "mede," she is the product of two objects, which the allegory conflates: the woman as object of desire; and the woman as exchanged object. This personification offers a naturalized representation of wealth (one that is alienated from its production) and a naturalized representation of woman (one that assumes women are all potential wives or whores). The question of agency is therefore also mystified: reward circulates without reference to its production, and Mede has no subjectivity, no agency, of her own. In sum, the model of the family that produces Mede emphatically casts her as object rather than subject of her actions. Mede-as-woman cannot exchange commodities herself, a fact that is brought into sharper focus when we compare her with Rosie the Regrator in Passus V (B V 211–25). Wife of Coueitise, Rosie is the domestic retailer working from within the family and the household as weaver, brewer, and cook—a familiar pattern of female work both in town and country. Langland deflects the issue of women's work onto Rosie and defers the problem of class difference by casting Mede as an aristocratic woman whose endowment is land (which she cannot own herself, although she may adminster it during her lifetime). In terms of the dual concepts of the family and the household that appear to underpin the gendered relations of production in feudalism, Mede is overdetermined as a symbol of patriarchal marriage and has no household from which to work.

There is one final irony. As a symbol of Mede's power to corrupt, Langland uses the narrative of the trial of Pees. Mede's greatest threat is to the king's authority, to the Law, and yet this is precisely where medieval women were at the greatest disadvantage. As Judith Bennett reminds us: "Countrywomen never served as reeves, townswomen never acted as mayors, and feudal women never went to parliament to advise their king" and, I might add, real medieval prostitutes were similarly powerless.[30] While it is therefore true that women's ability to influence the law was necessarily indirect, the fact that Mede is a product, not a producer, denies her any real power at all.[31]

The dangers are twofold: men's business is indifferent to its own relations of production and women's business is unavailable for analysis. As a result, Mede says nothing about women, though much about the attitudes that men have toward women. It comes, therefore, as no surprise to me that Mede is not married. Unmarried, she comes finally to represent all that men fear and desire most—the whore. After all, she behaves just like a woman, doesn't she?

Notes

1. Catharine A. MacKinnon, "Feminism, Marxism, Method, and the State: An Agenda for Theory," in *The 'SIGNS' Reader: Women, Gender & Scholarship*, ed. Elizabeth Abel and Emily K. Abel (Chicago: University of Chicago, 1983), 227–56 (at 252).

2. For discussion of women's agency and work without reference to class, see, for example, the essays collected in *Sisters and Workers in the Middle Ages*, ed. Judith M. Bennett et al. (Chicago: University of Chicago Press, 1989), especially 1–10 (Introduction) and "Crafts, Gilds, and Women in the Middle Ages: Fifty Years after Marian K. Dale," by Maryanne Kowaleski and Judith M. Bennett, 11–25. Martha C. Howell takes a similiar approach in *Women, Production, and Patriarchy in Late Medieval Cities* (Chicago: University of Chicago Press, 1986), where labor status take precedence over other markers of rank or status. Even those collections that are structured according to rough and ready definitions of female class do not adequately engage with the problems of definition; see, for example, *Women and Work in Pre-Industrial Europe*, ed. Barbara A. Hanawalt (Bloomington: Indiana University Press, 1986). The most recent and finest overview is that by Judith M. Bennett, "Medieval Women, Modern Women: Across the Great Divide," in *Culture and History 1350–1660: Essays on English Communities, Identities and Writing*, ed. David Aers (Detroit: Wayne State University Press, 1992), 147–75.

3. When I look at the broader contemporary political context of left-allianced politics and the feminist movement from the sixties onward, I see good grounds for skepticism. As is well known, mainstream socialist and Marxist movements tended to lose sight of women's concerns, which were hidden within conventional analyses of the class struggle as well as low priority on the various political agendas (where women were often bought off with glib and empty promises of liberation *after* the revolution-which-never-happened). The history of these bitter alliances reaches back to the nineteenth century and forward to our present: it is only too easy to see why the two "camps" circle each other warily. And yet, although feminist theory has concentrated on the limitations of a rapprochement between feminism and historical materialism, this fact alone reminds us just how closely interlinked these two "foes" remain. For useful introductions to the Marxist/feminist debate, see Michèle Barrett, *Women's Oppression Today: The Marxist/Feminist Encounter* (London: Verso, 1980, rev. 1988), 8–41; MacKinnon, "Feminism, Marxism, Method, and the State"; Juliet Mitchell, *Women: The Longest Revolution* (New York: Pantheon, 1966, repr. 1984), 19–54; and Sylvia Walby, *Theorizing Patriarchy* (Oxford: Blackwell, 1990), 1–24. A useful historical perspective is provided by Barbara Taylor, *Eve and the New Jerusalem: Socialism and Feminism in the Nineteenth Century* (New York: Pantheon, 1983). For pertinent comments on the problems of intersecting class and gender analysis in medieval literature, see Karma Lochrie's chapter in this volume.

4. One classic work rethinking feudalism is the collection of essays by Rodney Hilton, *Class Conflict and the Crisis of Feudalism* (London: Verso, 1985,

rev. 1990). See especially "Feudalism in Europe: Problems for Historical Materialists" (1–11), which assumes that the reproduction of the family was as much a part of the economic process as the production of crops. For a broader overview of feudalism from a materialist perspective, see Perry Anderson, *Passages from Antiquity to Feudalism* (London: Verso, 1974); and *Lineages of the Absolutist State* (London: Verso, 1974). The distinction between the family and the household is lucidly explicated by Martha Howell, *Women, Production, and Patriarchy in Late Medieval Cities*, 9–43.

5. Much valuable work on class conflict in feudalism reveals the extent to which struggle was inherent to feudalism, but there are few detailed studies of how far such resistance was a gendered activity. For a useful overview of conflict in medieval Europe, see Rodney Hilton, *Bond Men Made Free: Medieval Peasant Movements and the English Rising of 1381* (London: Temple Smith, 1973, repr. 1977); and *The English Peasantry in the Later Middle Ages* (Oxford: Clarendon, 1975), where pp. 95–110 address women villagers.

6. For examples of studies of women's work, see Judith M. Bennett, *Women in the Medieval English Countryside: Gender and Household in Brigstock before the Plague* (Oxford: Oxford University Press, 1987), and her "Medieval Women, Modern Women"; Martha C. Howell, *Women, Production, and Patriarchy in Late Medieval Cities;* Rodney Hilton, "Women Traders in Medieval England," repr. in *Class Conflict and the Crisis of Feudalism*, 132–42; and the relevant essays in *Women and Work in Pre-Industrial Europe*, ed. Barbara Hanawalt. For studies of gender conflict in written texts, see, for example, David Aers, *Community, Gender, and Individual Identity: English Writing 1360–1430* (London: Routledge, 1988); Sheila Delany, *Medieval Literary Politics: Shapes of Ideology* (Manchester: Manchester University Press, 1990); Carolyn Dinshaw, *Chaucer's Sexual Poetics* (Madison: University of Wisconsin Press, 1989). Gillian R. Overing has an important study of desire in her *Language, Sign, and Gender in* Beowulf (Carbondale: Southern Illinois University Press, 1990).

7. See *Women and Revolution: A Discussion of the Unhappy Marriage of Marxism and Feminism*, ed. Lydia Sargent (Boston: South End, 1981), especially Heidi Hartmann, "The Unhappy Marriage of Marxism and Feminism: Towards a More Progressive Union," 1–42.

8. I concentrate mainly on the B text of the poem. For editions, see George Kane, ed., Piers Plowman: *The A Version* (London: Athlone, 1960); Kane and E. Talbot Donaldson, ed., Piers Plowman: *The B Version* (London: Athlone, 1975); and Derek Pearsall, ed., Piers Plowman *by William Langland: An Edition of the C-Text* (London: Arnold, 1978).

9. In addition to Aers's *Community, Gender, and Individual Identity*, 20–72, see his *Chaucer, Langland and the Creative Imagination* (London: Routledge, 1980), especially 1–61. See also Britton J. Harwood, "The Plot of *Piers Plowman* and the Contradictions of Feudalism," in *Speaking Two Languages: Traditional Disciplines and Contemporary Theory in Medieval Studies*, ed. Allen J. Frantzen (Albany: SUNY Press, 1991), 91–114.

10. The main studies are : Anna P. Baldwin, *The Theme of Government in* Piers Plowman (Cambridge: Brewer, 1981); C. David Benson, "The Function of Lady Meed in *Piers Plowman*," *English Studies* 61 (1980): 193–205; T. P.

Dunning, Piers Plowman: *An Interpretation of the A-Text,* 2nd ed. rev. T. P. Dolan (Oxford: Clarendon Press, 1980), 48–84; Lavinia Griffiths, *Personification in* Piers Plowman (Cambridge: Brewer, 1985); A. G. Mitchell, *Lady Meed and the Art of* Piers Plowman, Chambers Memorial Lecture (London: Lewis, 1956); D. W. Robertson, Jr. and Bernard F. Huppé, Piers Plowman *and Scriptural Tradition* (Princeton: Princeton University Press, 1951), 49–71; and John A. Yunck, *The Lineage of Lady Meed: The Development of Mediaeval Venality Satire* (Notre Dame: University of Notre Dame Press, 1963).

11. Lavinia Griffiths explores this issue in *Personification in* Piers Plowman, 4–10 and 26–40.

12. For an example of a masculine "meed," see "Mede & Muche Thank," *Twenty-Six Political and Other Poems,* ed. J. Kail, EETS os 124 (London, 1904), 6–9. Money is personified as masculine in "Money, Money!," while "The Crowned King" draws on rhetoric similar to that of Langland's Meed; also for a male figure, see *Historical Poems of the XIVth and XVth Centuries,* ed. Rossell Hope Robbins (New York: Columbia University Press, 1959), 134–80 and 227–32.

13. Baldwin, *The Theme of Government in* Piers Plowman, 24–54.

14. Rodney Hilton offers a convenient summary in "Women Traders in Medieval England," 132–33.

15. C. David Benson, "The Function of Lady Meed in *Piers Plowman*" (which sees Mede as a type of Christ); Malcolm Godden, *The Making of* Piers Plowman (London: Longman, 1990); and A. G. Mitchell, *Lady Meed and the Art of* Piers Plowman.

16. Godden, *The Making of* Piers Plowman, 36.

17. The fact that "hor(e)" is itself ambiguous in Middle English is not beside the point: as the Middle English Dictionary points out, it can refer to moral foulness, filth, and corruption, a woman who prostitutes herself for money, and a woman who commits fornication or adultery (as in the case of Meed). The ambivalence expressed toward the medieval prostitute from the standpoint both of theory and praxis is discussed by James A. Brundage, "Prostitution in the Medieval Canon Law," and Ruth Mazo Karras, "The Regulation of Brothels in Later Medieval England," in *Sisters and Workers in the Middle Ages,* ed. Bennett et al., 79–99 and 100–34.

18. The psychological concept of overdetermination has been usefully applied to materialist analysis by Harriet Fraad, Stephen Resnick, and Richard Wolff, "For Every Knight in Shining Armor, There's a Castle Waiting to Be Cleaned: A Marxist-Feminist Analysis of the Household," *Rethinking Marxism* 2 (1989): 10–69. See also their response, "Class, Patriarchy, and Power: A Reply," *Rethinking Marxism* 3 (1990): 124–44.

19. From Marx, *Capital,* vol. 1, chap. 1, repr. in *The Portable Karl Marx,* ed. and trans. Eugene Kamenka (Harmondsworth: Penguin, 1983), 438.

20. Luce Irigaray, "Women on the Market," *This Sex Which Is Not One,* trans. Catherine Porter with Carolyn Burke (Ithaca: Cornell University Press, 1985), 170–91 (at 177).

21. I take the ambiguity of pronominal reference in Holy Church's reply to the dreamer's question to be central to the "confusion" that Meed produces:

"Loke [o]n þi left half, and lo where he stondeþ" (B II 5: with variants "sche" and "þei"). For discussion, see pp. 119–20.

22. The relevant discussions are Freud, "Fetishism," *The Standard Edition of the Complete Psychological Works of Sigmund Freud,* ed. and trans. James Strachey, vol. 23 (London: Hogarth, 1961), 149–58, where both the avowal and disavowal of the significance of the fetish is central to its structure, and Marx's interestingly analogous use of the same word in "The Fetishism of Commodities" in *The Portable Karl Marx,* 444–61. Gayatri Chakravorty Spivak stresses the analogy of money and the sign in writing in "Speculations on Reading Marx: After Reading Derrida," in *Post-Structuralism and the Question of History,* ed. Derek Attridge, Geoff Bennington, and Robert Young (Cambridge: Cambridge University Press, 1987), 30–62; see especially 32.

23. It is a commonplace of medieval grammar that the terms 'masculine' and 'feminine' (for grammatical gender) are derived from sex, that which is male and female and is capable of generation in nature: see, for example, Priscian, *Institutionum Grammaticarum,* ed. Martin Hertz; *Grammatici Latini,* ed. H. Keil, vol. 2 (Leipzig: Teubner, 1855), 141: "genera enim dicuntur a generando proprie quae generare possunt, quae sunt masculinum et femininum." See also the suggestive comments on the relationship between grammar and lineage in R. Howard Bloch, *Etymologies and Genealogies: A Literary Anthropology of the French Middle Ages* (Chicago: University of Chicago Press, 1983 repr. 1986), 83–87. The association persists long after the medieval period, of course. For discussion, see Dennis E. Baron, *Grammar and Gender* (New Haven: Yale University Press, 1986), 91–111.

24. For a related discussion of this passage, see Margaret Amassian and James Sadowsky, "Mede and Mercede: A Study of the Grammatical Metaphor in *Piers Plowman,* C: IV: 335–409," *NM* 72 (1971): 457–76.

25. This is not the case with peasant families, where descent was bilateral and inheritance thus much less clearly defined. For discussion, see Barbara A. Hanawalt, *The Ties That Bound: Peasant Families in Medieval England* (New York: Oxford University Press, 1986), 67–89.

26. Note the further mystification in C II 80, "and for here richesse."

27. Or, as Irigaray states in "Women on the Market," *This Sex Which Is Not One,* 186: "Prostitution amounts to *usage that is exchanged.* Usage that is not merely potential: it has already been realized. The woman's body is valuable because it has already been used. In the extreme case, the more it has served, the more it is worth. Not because its natural assets have been put to use this way, but, on the contrary, because its nature has been 'used up,' and has become once again no more than a vehicle for relations between men."

28. My reading of Mede thus complements Harwood's far more detailed analysis of the contradictions of feudalism in "The Plot of *Piers Plowman*"; see especially his concluding remarks, 112: ". . . in all the thousands of lines in *Piers,* for example, not one peasant is represented as leaving a manor so that he might work for wages. . . ."

29. In addition to the studies of women's work in notes 2 and 6 above, see also Sylvia L. Thrupp, *The Merchant Class of Medieval London* (Ann Arbor: University of Michigan Press, 1948, repr. 1989), 169–74; and Marian K. Dale,

"The London Silkwomen of the Fifteenth Century," repr. in *Sisters and Workers in the Middle Ages,* ed. Bennett et al., 26–38. The over-optimism of some of these studies is stressed by Judith M. Bennett, "Medieval Women, Modern Women," 150–62.

30. Bennett, *Women in the English Medieval Countryside,* 185. See also Rodney Hilton's pertinent comments on the importance of jurisdiction in feudal political domination in "Feudalism in Europe: Problems for Historical Materialists," *Class Conflict and the Crisis of Feudalism,* 2. For discussion of the powerlessness of prostitutes, see the articles by Brundage and Karras in note 17.

31. See the suggestive comments about women and the law in Bennett's *Women in the English Medieval Countryside,* 21–32, which stress that even indirect influence by women was more limited than by men. One aristocratic woman, Alice Perrers, did exert considerable influence on men's business, but Langland's Mede has little real narrative influence on her king and, in my analysis of her as product, could not have had influence. For a relevant discussion, see Anna P. Baldwin, "The Historical Context," *A Companion to* Piers Plowman, ed. John A. Alford (Berkeley: University of California Press, 1988), 79–80.

The Pardoner's Tale, the Pervert, and the Price of Order in Chaucer's World

* * *

Allen J. Frantzen

Criticism engaging both gender and class emphasizes the personal in the professional, the relationship between what we do and who we are.[1] Such criticism involves two "categories of difference," Elaine Showalter writes, that "structure our lives and texts."[2] Another of these structuring categories is academic specialization. I usually work in Old English; like many Anglo-Saxonists who also teach Middle English texts, I find myself feeling somewhat insecure when discussing Chaucer outside the classroom. One venerable way of dealing with insecurity in public is the use of an anecdote to preface one's paper. Gayle Margherita had explicated the division of the anecdote from the paper, contrasting experience (what I did) with authority (what I know), the Real with the theoretical.[3] Essential to the occasion of the paper's delivery—and perhaps to the paper itself—the anecdote creates a contradiction: it speaks what one's paper supposedly cannot say. Yet the anecdote is an anecdote nonetheless; from the Greek *anekdotos,* meaning 'unpublished', 'not given out', it is not, after all, part of the paper. When I wrote this chapter on the Pardoner, I remembered an anecdote that addresses insecurity. About the personal in the professional, and also about money and sex, this anecdote is appropriate to the Pardoner, in whom personal and professional interests intersect.

Minutes before I read a paper at the New Chaucer Society meeting in 1988, John Fisher approached, smiling benevolently, and put his arm around my shoulder. "Don't worry, Allen," he said, "they found your checks." "What checks?" I asked. "My traveller's checks?" Patting my jacket pocket nervously, I found it lighter by several hundred dollars. Happy though I was to know that I would get my money back, I was more than a little shaken to realize I had not known it was missing. This seemed to be an American Express commercial in reverse. Can you grieve before you realize that you have sustained a loss, and after it has been recovered? Once again possessed of my funds, and suddenly very concerned about my paper, I found myself in the conference room, wondering if I should work a comment—an anecdote, that is—about this episode into my opening paragraph in order to relieve my nervousness. I did not do so, but I should have. Sitting in the front row, listening to David Wallace introduce the session, I anxiously sought reassurance that I was in charge. I glanced down at my paper and was shocked to see my Jockey shorts instead. I hastily closed my zipper and went to the podium. Having found myself unbuttoned and unzipped, I was also unnerved. My paper was shaky for reasons having nothing to do with my argument about the *Parliament of Fowls*.

What reminded me of this intrusion of the personal into the professional was my response to the vulnerability of the Pardoner. Like him, we try to keep our valuables buttoned up and close to the body. Britton J. Harwood has recently observed that the Pardoner is surrounded by closed containers and secrets. Harwood sees the Pardoner in terms of a "dialectic between the closed chest and the open one" that generates a "dialectic between a pardoner who makes money by exploiting closed chests and the pardoner who opens up his secrets." Quoting Gaston Bachelard, Harwood reminds us that secrets retain value only so long as they are protected: "there will always be more things in a closed, than in an open, box."[4] I had failed rather conspicuously in guarding my enclosures, having left both my pocket and my zipper open and unprotected. Exposure, whether personal or professional, can be expensive, as the Pardoner's case demonstrates. He opens the box that hides certain economies essential to medieval Christianity, and for exposing these order-maintaining principles he pays a great price. My aim is to consider the Pardoner's exposures in terms of the interdependent forces known as the "three estates," structures that enclose secrets of gender and class in the Pardoner's tale.

The Pardoner is situated at a point of exchange in terms of both gender and class. His profession involves the exchange of surplus extracted from those who work for a living—sheep farmers and others mentioned in his prologue—and given to those who pray. The Pardoner is engaged in a kind of commerce: he creates a lack when he reminds his audience of its sinfulness and then fills that lack by selling indulgences. The ecclesiastical hierarchy claims surplus literally as its due; it is God-taken, rather than God-given. This process of the creation, extraction, and re-distribution of surplus engages gender only indirectly. Gender is sub-sumed into categories of production and consumption, but the categories of male and female typicality are unavoidably mixed by the Pardoner's own confusing sexual semiosis. The vagueness of the Par-doner's sexuality emphasizes his vulnerable position between the sex-ualized male and sexualized female; simultaneously it calls attention to his ambiguous gender identity. Either "a geldyng or a mare," accord-ing to the narrator (General Prologue, I.691), the Pardoner is described in the *Riverside Chaucer* as a "mannish woman," possibly homosex-ual, "feminine," hermaphroditic, a eunuch, possibly a homosexual eu-nuch, and sexually abnormal.[5] It is not necessary to insist that he is homosexual or to identify the Pardoner as gay; to do so is to assume (without evidence) that such a category constitutes medieval identity when it seems, rather, to describe acts performed by certain persons that contributed to their identity but did not define them. Whatever he is, however, the Pardoner is not an FFM—a fully functioning male. Now the three men in his tale are FFMs, that is certain, sexualized to the hilt, and they thus define one end of the sexual polarity. They con-sume without producing; the Pardoner does both, although what he pro-duces, we will see, has little but verbal substance. To move to the other end of the sexual scale that measures the Pardoner's gender identity, we must look to—indeed, look for—the women.

Few women appear in this text, and the work assigned to them is not obvious. The Pardoner's jokes aside, women are not seen primarily as sexual temptations. He assails many vices, but among them lechery is merely annexed to gluttony. Accordingly, women are merely annexed to the Pardoner's main concerns, which are the exchange of goods and the accumulation of wealth. Regarded chiefly as possessions who violate the rights of ownership by committing adultery, women are introduced through and annexed to men. We meet women in church after we meet their husbands and are reminded of the systems that keep women in their place. "Goode men," the Pardoner begins, "taak of my wordes keep" (VI.352). He then offers them a sheep bone that will give heal-ing powers to well water; if the "good-man" or head of household who owns animals drinks from this water every week, his animals will mul-tiply (VI.365). Speaking next to "sires," the Pardoner claims that the blessed water will cure a man of jealous fits; even if he knows for a fact that the man's wife is unfaithful and has "taken prestes two or thre," her husband will no more "his wyf mystriste" (VI.369). Only then are women addressed directly. "Goode men and wommen, o thyng warne I yow" (VI.377), says the Pardoner: anyone guilty of "synne horrible, that he / Dar nat, for shame, of it yshryven be," or any woman who cheats on her husband, cannot benefit from his relics (VI.379–80).[6] The Pardoner acknowledges the man as head of the household and places the woman among the man's possessions. Her infidelities, the Pardoner implies, are not serious "defaute[s]"; for they can be concealed by the same water that heals animal illnesses, and everyone will be better off. The wife can continue (to enjoy?) her adulteries; her husband will no longer mind them; and priests, obviously, also fare well. At the end of the prologue we find another woman, "the povereste wydwe in a village" who is deprived of the protection of a man. But she has food and clothing, the Pardoner says, so let her beware, for he will have her wool, cheese, wheat, and money, even though it means that her children starve. It is not only women he would rob of life's barest necessities: he would take the same from "the povereste page" (VI.448–51). The Pardoner wants to extract *everything* from the system of production, including what others need for subsistence, not just their surplus.

Although the Pardoner links both men and women to production, women—such as the poor widow—are particularly associated with food. Some women who hang about the tavern in the tale are dancing girls, but among them are fruit-sellers ("tombesteres," "frutesteres," VI.477–80). Other women are shadowy presences; Eve is mentioned as the "wyf" of Adam but she is not named (VI.505), and other references are even more cursory. The mother ("dame") of one of the men's knaves has warned the boy to be prepared for Death (VI.684), and "Seinte Marie" is the tavern keeper's oath (VI.685). There is, unforgettably, in a scene that Chaucer plays like a violin, the "leeve mooder" (VI.731) of earth who will not admit the Old Man to his final resting place. The association of women with food, a link that resurfaces when the three men find gold, is a significant feature of the feminine in this tale. Production was still centered in the fourteenth-century English household, and women were clearly engaged in it in a real economic sense, although it is not to the women but to the men that the Pardoner appeals as he speaks.[7]

If, in the Pardoner's tale, gendered differences between the male and the female are mere subtext, class standing counts for a great deal. Class appears in the tale in the form of the "trifunctional" model of medieval estates: those who fight for all, those who work, and those who pray. Georges Duby has articulated the development of this model in the early medieval period, stressing (but not explaining) its curious prominence in Anglo-Saxon records.[8] Paul Strohm has reminded us that this model was an ideological commonplace long before Chaucer's time, and that the gaps and lines dividing these three estates had long since been filled in with a plethora of new classes such as the managerial class that was among those which Chaucer inhabited. Duby shows that the model, never a cultural constant, changed in both form and significance in phase after phase of struggle between monarchical and monastic power. So it is hardly to be expected that Henry de Bracton's thirteenth-century description of the three estates should be "descriptive of a thirteenth- or fourteenth-century English state of affairs." Instead, Strohm emphasizes that the model's "ideological work is accomplished in part through 'illusion': its omission of classes outside the model of the three estates, its relative neglect of social interdependence, its suggestion that the system it describes exists beyond time and change."[9] But, as a cultural myth "beyond time and change," the model retains its power to identify and enforce categories of difference. Duby makes the power of the model clear as a force *in* space and time, and I would not wish to suggest that if we see the model as figurative, as a myth, its powers are lessened. In the Pardoner's tale, I believe, Chaucer provisionally negates this model and demonstrates, through the fates of the three men and the Pardoner himself, the gratuitous but deeply satisfying destruction of those who depart from the order it dictates.

The negative image of the trifunctional model, which asserts the interdependence of the three orders, is the trio of tavern sins. The need for rule is mocked by gambling, which is play based on chance and misrule. The need to work is mocked by gluttons who consume but do not produce. And the need for prayer is mocked by those who swear. Such oaths as "Goddes armes" (VI.692), a pun on God's two arms and on His "arms" (weapons), express rebellion against prayer in a war of wills: rather than submit to God's will, the three men do verbal violence to His person. These negations are even more complex, as swearing on God's "arms" suggests: swearing in this sense inverts fighting, just as gambling (dicing), which denies providential order, inverts prayer. Swearing leads to lawlessness, and the great mission of the three figures in the tale, their assault on death, is a culmination of their threefold perversion of social order and is their most powerful assault on it. For it is ultimately the presence of death—that is, the demand of the immortal on the mortal—that manages the three estates: the disciplines of work, prayer, and rule are all necessary because only in a world ordered by them can life be directed toward the everlasting good and away from the everlasting evil. Without such guidance there is no salvation.

Another way to analyze the three estates is to say that, underneath the ideological, theological superstructure, material reality masters the situation. The Church competes for control of material wealth with the laity, claiming that it needs this wealth to support its own activities, especially the ministries of prayer and service to the sick and the poor. Actually, Chaucer shows us that the clergy, having convinced the working classes that their salvation required surrendering their goods to the Church, too often kept the material benefits for themselves. The extraction of surplus from labor was rationalized as the price of religion, the price of the Church, and the price of order. But it was not surplus that kept this ordering machine in place, nor was it the threat of death; rather, the machine was kept in place by *lack*. Social interdependence was and is based on installing a sense of lack in the subject: no estate is complete, for each requires another to make it whole. Lack drives the system; lack reminds people that they depend on others, on other estates; lack keeps the system in place by keeping people in their places.

We see the danger of the tavern sins, then, because they direct the flow of surplus away from the Church, where it belongs, to human consumption in pleasure. We know the vast sermon literature denouncing these sins, warning that the glutton threatens both social order and the common weal.[10] In the Pardoner's tale, we find that those who enjoy surplus do not properly pay for it: they do not demonstrate the lack that ought to keep them in their place. The three men seem to have no employment, although they certainly have a life. "Yonge folk that haunteden folye," they make a habit of dice, brothels, and taverns; they enjoy themselves day and night—which means they can hardly work—and they regularly drink and eat too much (VI.463–71). Their desire could be described in the language of Klaus Theweleit, in *Male Fantasies*, as "revolutionary": it wants what it wants, and it does not need an end, goal, or identity to direct it (1:270).[11]

For their excesses, the three ruffians are not punished but instead rewarded; their free and irresponsible behavior leads to the promise of even greater freedom when they find gold under the tree. Having done no work, having pursued their own will against God's (their mission in slaying Death), and having rebelled against all productive order, even against the Old Man's warning, they are, suddenly, terribly rich, able to spend as freely as they get, suddenly free to make their own world. Even worse, they know it.

> "This tresor hath Fortune unto us yiven,
> In myrthe and joliftee oure lyf to lyven,
> And lightly as it comth, so wol we spende." (VI.779–781)

This is fantasy; it is what Deleuze and Guattari call "deterritorialization," the "opening up of new possibilities for desiring-production across the 'body [without] organs.' " The countermovement that is required to check this freedom is "reterritorialization," which is "the mobilization of dominant forces to prevent new productive possibilities from becoming new human freedoms."[12] In the language used so creatively by Theweleit, the stream of freedom, of new possibilities, must be *dammed up* before it flows out of control (1.229–435). How is this freedom reterritorialized, and how does it relate to the Pardoner? Chaucer knows and shows the way: the freedom—and the free men—must be damned.

Having prospered against every bit of advice and restriction the Church could muster to discipline the faithful, the three men cannot be allowed to get away with their success. The delay in their gratification, the development of their plan to cart off the money, depends on the sudden intervention of commonplace morality. The men must scheme to take the gold because they do not want to be thought of as *arrant* thieves: "Men wolde seyn that we were theves stronge" (VI.789). Others must not think that this gold was taken in *open* violation of others' property rights. Caught with stolen wealth—they could not reasonably explain how they came by it—the three men would be subject to summary execution; as one of them observed, they could be hanged (VI.790).[13] They are, we begin to see, not so free after all. Thereafter the binding power of lack, essential to the estates model, emerges to undo their fantasy. The three divide into two camps. One of them is feminized: by being designated as the youngest, he is made the lackey and is sent off for food and wine. The two who remain plot against him. This itself is a smug allegory of social disorder that pits the two who rule against the one who works and thereby reorganizes the dynamics of the plot. We see the importance of the trifunctional model, the threefold nature of which disguises the binary opposition between the ruled and the rulers: when the three are reduced to two, the illusion of harmony is shattered. The division of the three men among themselves is correctly seen in the critical tradition as a parody of a cooperative community, a self-contained world ordered (and disordered) according to the three men's desires. The end of that world is brought about by the same forces that will, if they are not regulated, destroy the world of the estates as they are properly constituted. We know this lesson: either the estates work together or they perish.

The phony vulnerability of the three men is demonstrated in the seemingly neat mechanism that ends the tale itself. The two kill the youngest one, but even dead he kills them right back. These murders are carefully planned, but his mayhem is not sufficiently motivated by the materials of the plot. Having found wealth by chance, the three men do not, actually, all have to die: the youngest is murdered, but why do the two who remain both take bottles with poison in them? After all, there is one bottle without poison, and one of them could have drunk from it. But "par cas," by accident, both drink poisoned wine. By accident? This final death does not happen by accident any more than the Knight is selected as first teller "by aventure, by sort, or cas" (I.844). Indeed, it is the *same* force of social order operating in the General Prologue that demands the men's doom here. They die as a result of the need of a dominant ideology (endorsing the trifunctional model) to dam up their freedom from work, from guilt, from obligations to the wider social world, and to damn them.

We know of course that "death" of a kind awaits the Pardoner. But this is not to say that his sins are quite the same as those of the three men. Gluttony and avarice are common to them, but the Pardoner negates the trifunctional model in a different way. He works while they gamble, and his curses are different, too. He would rather damn the faithful than save them (their salvation, fortunately, does not depend on his intention but on their own in submitting to him and on their belief in his holy power). Like the three men in his tale, he accomplishes the opposite of what the orders of society should accomplish: he promotes sin rather than prayer or grace and substitutes the chaos of immorality and duplicity for governance in the name of the Church. Unlike the three men, however, the Pardoner does not merely consume; rather, he produces speech and salvific opportunities for the faithful. What he consumes is different from what he produces: he takes the fruit of the labors of others in exchange for his own labor, but its fruits are questionable. Because he both produces (words) and consumes (goods), however, his productivity is sexualized differently from and in between that of other men and the women in the text. This is how his gender is related to his function within the trifunctional scheme.

The Pardoner plainly and indeed gleefully exposes the social facts of Christianity. Religion, he shows, is a swindle in which the Church consumes—acquires pennies—and without producing much (in his case, hollow pardons). He parodies the exchange of material goods for spiritual gain. In exchange for pence or bartered goods, he cheats his customers twice: their cattle will not fatten and their souls will not go to heaven. Like the three men in his tale, he has mastered the art of getting something for nothing. But even though he uses the language of guilt (he knows he is "ful vicious," for example [VI.459]), and even though he has mastered the discourses of the preacher, he does not believe what he says to others. Worse than his fake pardons is the power of his speech, which creates a fake religion of his own as powerful as real religion. Real religion makes believers free, although not all believers are equally free; so does the Pardoner's religion, which also redirects and redefines as surplus what is necessary for subsistence. His preaching is "for to make hem free / To yeven hir pens, and namely unto me" (VI.401–2). This preaching also makes *him* free, makes him rich, and has opened a world of new possibilities of pleasure for him. From the perspective of any social order, this is terrifying; it is the power that Carolyn Dinshaw calls the Pardoner's "disruptive possibility" as a false preacher.[14] It means that someone can be free and happy outside the system. And, if so, that there is no reason for others not to join him, provided they are as willing and able as he is to constitute a self-contained, self-directed world and possess its center. The Pardoner's religion is a world in which the strong prey on the weak, in which those with wit exploit the witless, in which wealth is transferred from the latter to the former under the guise of security, safety, and assurances of mutual prosperity. This is, of course, quite a familiar world: it is the world of medieval religion made small, one little world and also an everywhere.

The site of the Pardoner's escape to freedom, flaunted here in what I grant is a shocking manner, is the tavern (I accept that he speaks in such a setting; I know this is contested).[15] The vile attack on his sexuality at the end of the story is usually attributed to this implication of

inns in sins. Why does the Pardoner ask Harry, the innkeeper, of all
people, for money? Some argue that the Pardoner is drunk, and drunkenness, a fourteenth-century preacher said, in one of the Church's numerous denunciations of the tavern sins, left man dead in dung.[16] Harry
leaves us with death in dung, too: an image of the Pardoner's absent sex
organs "shryned in a hogges toord." The Pardoner's manliness, his
missing sexual power, is juxtaposed with his hollow "relikes," with his
own dung (the "paint" of "thy fundement" [VI.950]); its "seintuarie"
is the dung of the animal that symbolizes gluttony. Here Chaucer does
the unthinkable: he reminds us that man is born "inter feces et urinas,"
juxtaposing the excretory with the sexual, waste with pleasure, death
with birth.[17]

After years of teaching Chaucer I could barely discuss Harry's base
but extremely powerful juxtaposition of the glutton's waste with male
sexual power. For a while I thought that this positioning of the sexual in
the excremental evoked anal intercourse, a horror—homosexual or heterosexual—abominated by the Church. Of late, I have come to a different view of Harry's shrine of feces for the Pardoner's testicles.
Harry seems to take from the Pardoner what he does not have—that is,
he identifies the Pardoner's *lack,* the thing he does not have. Theweleit
describes lack, at one point, as "the incapacity to experience others except through fear, deceit, mistrust, or domination" (1.373).[18] The Pardoner's preaching "for hate" would seem to qualify as a reaction to
lack (VI.410–11), which seems to have been installed in him sexually.
His recourse to fear and deceit as means to domination is self-evident.
Conscious that one lacks, one struggles to possess whatever makes one-
self complete. But there is no desire for women or men driving the Pardoner, although he uses women to mediate between men and materials.
Since he is not sexualized in terms of gender roles, his desires fall outside them.

What he lacks is neither sexual fulfillment nor material riches. Instead, what he lacks is *lack itself.* What does this man need except to
talk? His means of satisfaction is neither his hands nor his sex organs
(he will not do manual labor or beg, VI.443–45) but an organ more
powerful than his penis or his hands: his tongue. For him, Dinshaw suggests, language serves "as a substitute for his literally or figuratively
absent genitals and for what that absence represents." For her this missing thing is "a Golden Age," a time in which self was not separated
from other.[19] But I see no need in the Pardoner for a utopia. In his approach to Harry, it seems as if the Pardoner cannot control his tongue

or the desire it serves. But this is an inadequate explanation, for the Pardoner is a skilled speaker. The reason nobody can explain *why* he does *what* he does is that there is no good reason *within the world of the text* for it. The Pardoner must make a mistake, but not because anything in his psychology demands it. As Pearsall says, he shows no signs of the psychological complexity that one admires in the Wife of Bath, no consciousness of conflicting motives, no urge to destroy himself.[20] The Pardoner must make this mistake because ideology demands that he be "reterritorialized": he cannot be as free as he claims to be. Thus, as if *bound* (obliged, perhaps by himself) to prove he is as good a crook as he says, the Pardoner provokes Harry's wrath and is destroyed.

In part this reterritorialization is necessary because the Pardoner is a sexual misfit. How does someone sexually configured like the Pardoner, either gelding or mare, figure into the economics of signification? A stable feature of feminist criticism, the economics of signification are most recently employed in Dinshaw's discussion of women and economic exchange.[21] With the help of Luce Irigaray, we can use the Pardoner to reconfigure Dinshaw's analysis in terms of homosexuality. Luce Irigaray asserts that

> the labor force and its products . . . are the object of transactions among men and men alone. This means that the *very possibility of a sociocultural order requires homosexuality* as its organizing principle. (Her emphasis)[22]

Judith Butler describes Irigaray's construct as a "masculinist signifying economy."[23] Since this economy is "masculine," and based on homosocial relations, male homosexuality, which includes the father-son relationship that guarantees "the transmission of patriarchal power and its laws, its discourse, its social structures," has to be suppressed. Homosexual relations must remain "in the realm of pretense" and can only be practiced in language; if they are practiced in any other way they would bring the symbolic order to an end. Irigaray continues:

> The "other" homosexual relations, masculine ones, are just as subversive [i.e., as that of father and son], so they too are forbidden. Because they openly interpret the law according to which society operates, they threaten in fact to shift the horizon of the law. (193)

Irigaray's analysis, it seems to me, has implications for my thesis about the Pardoner and institutional religion. The Pardoner exposes how the

system works and so subverts it, or at least threatens to "openly interpret the law according to which society operates" (according to which
the Church manages society's production, that is).

But it is not, finally, the Pardoner's sexuality that Harry wants to
attack. What Harry wants to destroy is the Pardoner's lack of lack,
his sufficiency of self. It is not that Harry names the Pardoner's testicles, makes them vividly present and destroys them, that causes this
annihilation, but rather that he *soils* them. Harry's real weapon is filth,
which we can define as "anything that impinges on the tidy insularity
of a person, on the person's anxiously guarded autonomy" (Theweleit
quoting Christian Enzenberger, 1.385). This disturbing juxtaposition
of sexual organs and animal excrement requires comment. In his discussion of medieval laws prohibiting sodomy, Arthur N. Gilbert notes
that the Church was disturbed by "the admission that the living body
constantly enacts the drama of death in its physical functions." "Excrement," he writes, "was always the clearest and most persistent reminder of the fate of man" and also "a symbol of evil, darkness,
death, and rebellion against the moral order." What Gilbert delicately
calls "the anal function" was an unwelcome reminder that humans
were connected "to the sheep, the dog, and the goat."[24] The reminder
is all the more graphic in the Pardoner's case, and all the more unwelcome, because Harry describes a pig's excrement as a "shrine" for—
as a body for—sex organs. Harry's offensive comment dirties the
Pardoner by linking sexual functions with excretory functions—his
own and an animal's—and reminding his audience that for people like
the Pardoner sexual acts could be associated with death and waste
rather than with life and creation.

The Pardoner is "reterritorialized" and his autonomy is revoked
when his insularity is violated, when his testicles are imaged as en-
shrined in animal excrement (his own excrement mentioned just sec-
onds earlier), as if neatness and sexual power defined him. Let us recall
that one of the three men, suddenly worried about being soiled (i.e., by
being called thieves), comes to realize the danger that their lawlessness
invites. Like "the proudeste of thise riotoures three" (VI.716), the Pardoner is supposedly brought down to earth, cut down to size. But this
is no fastidious Absolon from the Miller's world. The Pardoner is not
afraid to get dirty; nor is he worried about exposure (that is, about his
reputation), for he exposes himself. His end, like that of the three men,
is made too easy.

Chaucer could not conclude with Harry's outburst—the host swears and threatens the misrule of real physical violence—because it is itself disorderly. Of course Chaucer frequently does allow those who work to deliver the comeuppance to those who pervert religious duties (old Thomas, the old woman in the Friar's tale, and other honest layfolk). But the class conspiracy here calls for more class. And so enters the Knight, who notices that the pilgrims are laughing at what I have called unthinkable. In the words of countless critics and teachers, the knight "restores order." As Strohm states, the knight's intervention prevents "a schism between the community and its most precariously situated member" (156). And as Pearsall writes, "For all readers there seems to be the consciousness of a challenge to rescue the Pardoner from moral responsibility for his depravity, to enter psychological pleas for mitigation, and to re-enroll him in the margins of humanity" (94).

Let us resist these impulses. Having created a character whose will so powerfully exposes the weaknesses of the ecclesiastical system and its corruption, Chaucer had no choice but to assert his own will, at the *narrative* level, against the Pardoner. Chaucer silences him and gives the knight credit for "restoring" order (it was always there in the good old days). The pilgrims may laugh to see the Pardoner's sexual lack ridiculed and his tongue silenced. But I read their laughter less as ridicule than as relief that the flow of his dangerous words has been dammed up. And yet his humiliation was not necessary, for the Pardoner's invitation summoned his listeners to a freedom that none of them wants to take seriously. He openly interprets the law for them; he openly interprets the ecclesiastical, financial nexus that traps them; he offers to set them free.

Deleuze and Guattari explain that the neurotic, the pervert, and the psychotic react differently to the process of reterritorialization as they define themselves "in terms of modern territorialities." The neurotic is trapped "within the residual or artificial territorialities" of society, but the pervert—I would place the Pardoner in this category—"is someone who takes the artifice seriously and plays the game to the hilt," constructing territorialities, "infinitely more artificial than the ones that society offers us, totally artificial new families, secret lunar societies."[25] Harry, I submit, is the neurotic, as many of the Canterbury pilgrims are, trapped like him by the territorialities and the confines of ecclesiastical and financial networks. But the Pardoner, the pervert, is not. He creates his own networks and strategies for confin-

ing—for reterritorializing—others. He shows the pilgrims the operations of the system with complete clarity and, unforgivably, suggests
that their privileged place in society is in part an illusion. They are not
duped by *his* machinations, of course, for he has exposed his tech-
niques; but the true believers among them may suspect that they are
duped by the larger machinations of the system that remains hidden
from view.

Harry and the Knight (another neurotic) need to keep the system in
place. The Pardoner, of course, shares this need, but for different reasons. He refigures the system in his own perverted world, which is not
a secret lunar society but a one-man road show, an act, a performance
in which he dares to show that the individual can ape the institution's
work. His freedom to do so, to "[play] the game to the hilt," exposes
the marriage of money and religion that the whole medieval world, it
seems, needed to believe in but dared not look at.

Is the Pardoner's gender ambiguity at least partly responsible for his
freedom to parody the system in his own person? Butler reminds us that
neither sex nor gender is a transhistorical category and that it is "impossible to separate out 'gender' from the political and cultural intersections in which it is invariably produced and maintained" (4). The
Pardoner's gender can nonetheless be gauged in relation to the extremes
his text offers. We see him negotiating the masculine and the feminine
in the signifying economy, and likewise negotiating the world of true
religion and his own world of fake, perverted religion. Free of the po-
larized limits of male/female and belief in salvation or damnation, he is
free to make up limits of his own and powerful enough to impose them
on others. The extreme violence and crudity of Harry's response to this
bold freedom (and Chaucer's, too) is usually interpreted as the price the
Pardoner pays for going too far; I would say, to the contrary, that the
frightened and frightening responses demonstrated in this episode are
the measure of the Pardoner's success.

When I developed this argument about the Pardoner and the price
he pays for violating the order of the medieval Christian world, I
had not read Jonathan Dollimore's remarkable *Sexual Dissidence,*
an extended discussion of perversity and trangressive desire from
Augustine to Wilde and from Freud to Foucault. Much of what Dollimore writes about the pervert seems to apply directly to the Pardoner.
Perversion, Dollimore suggests, embodies a paradox: "[W]hatever a
culture designates as alien, utterly other, and incommensurably different is rarely and perhaps never so." Dollimore quotes Jonathan Culler's

claim that "Understanding the marginal or deviant term becomes a condition of understanding the supposedly prior term."[26] Hence understanding the Pardoner's perversity is part of understanding the Christian values his prologue and tale so bitterly expose. I read Dollimore's book too late to allow me to rethink the role of perversity in my chapter but not too late to allow me to include his comment on the intersection of medieval and modern ideas. "Sexual perversion is a modern notion," he writes, "hardly more than a century old, and grew from medical discourses which were effectively replacing religious ones." He continues:

> In keeping with that change, we are told, sexual deviation comes to be understood as an illness or a congenital abnormality rather than a sin. However, structures developed within the concept of the sinfully perverse persist into modern theories of the sexually perverse. That much has become apparent in the demonizing, punitive response to the catastrophe of AIDS. . . . (144)

To stigmatize difference as perversity is the first step to demonizing it. Does Harry demonize the Pardoner? Have critics followed the Host in this act? If we suspend the identification of difference as perversity, what can the Pardoner teach us about the ordering forces of Chaucer's world? Quite a lot, I think. Freud, Dollimore writes, "argues not just that civilization understands itself through perversion, but that the latter, via sublimation, remains integral to the former" (183). The Pardoner is integral, not marginal; his tale leads us to the heart of medieval Christianity.

My analysis of the Pardoner could be construed as a celebration of his perverse powers. I do not commend his excesses, however, any more than I would suggest that he functioned in a fully developed capitalist world of production and consumption. I do find a mix of Marxism and gender criticism—the language of Deleuze and Guattari, of Theweleit, Butler, and others, including Dollimore—helpful in grasping Chaucer's use of the Pardoner. Complex and confusing, the Pardoner was and is a double threat. It is no wonder that Chaucer, along with his pilgrims, was eager to see him silenced. For the Pardoner exposed, did he not, the death-threatening, life-denying, spirit-crushing construction of lack, the safe house of the Everlasting Nay in which religion locked the pleasures and the freedom it feared to let loose in the world.

Notes

1. I thank James W. Earl, Britton J. Harwood, Gillian R. Overing, John W. Tanke, and David Wallace for generous comments on and criticisms of this essay.

2. Elaine Showalter, "Introduction: The Rise of Gender," in *Speaking of Gender*, ed. Showalter (New York: Routledge, 1989), 3.

3. Gayle Margherita, "Medieval Studies and the Politics of Literary Theory," read at the Twenty-sixth International Congress on Medieval Studies, Kalamazoo, May 1991. Her paper refers to Joel Fineman's justly famous essay "The History of the Anecdote."

4. Britton J. Harwood, "Chaucer's Pardoner: The Dialectics of Inside and Outside," *PQ* 67 (1988): 409–22.

5. Larry D. Benson, ed., *The Riverside Chaucer* (New York: Houghton Mifflin, 1987), 824–25. All quotations are taken from this edition. Chaucerian discourse on the Pardoner is extensive. Important recent readings include Carolyn Dinshaw, *Chaucer's Sexual Poetics* (Madison: University of Wisconsin Press, 1989), 156–86; Lee Patterson, *Chaucer and the Subject of History* (Madison: University of Wisconsin Press, 1991), 367–421; H. Marshall Leicester, Jr., *The Disenchanted Self: Representing the Subject in the* Canterbury Tales (Berkeley: University of California Press, 1990), 35–64 and 161–77; Glenn Burger, "Kissing the Pardoner," *PMLA* 107 (1992): 1143–56.

6. For a discussion of this passage and its relation to the famous "Love that dare not speak its name," Lord Alfred Douglas's phrase in reference to Oscar Wilde, see Monica McAlpine, "The Pardoner's Homosexuality and How it Matters," *PMLA* 95 (1980): 8–22, see 15–16.

7. See Barbara Hanawalt, ed., *Women and Work in Pre-Industrial Europe* (Bloomington: Indiana University Press, 1986). I thank David Wallace for his comments on this point.

8. Georges Duby, *The Three Orders: Feudal Society Imagined,* trans. Arthur Goldhammer (Chicago: University of Chicago Press, 1980); see 99, 102–105, 108 on the Anglo-Saxon evidence.

9. Paul Strohm, *Social Chaucer* (Cambridge: Harvard University Press, 1989), 3.

10. See the many references in G. R. Owst's discussion of gluttony in *Literature and Pulpit in Medieval England* (Cambridge, 1933; repr. Oxford: Blackwell, 1966), 436–47; on the "common weal," see 432–33.

11. Klaus Theweleit, *Male Fantasies,* 2 vols. trans. Stephen Conway (Minneapolis: University of Minnesota Press, 1987), 1:270. Further references (all to volume 1) are given in the text.

12. Gilles Deleuze and Felix Guattari, *Anti-Oedipus: Capitalism and Schizophrenia,* trans. Robert Hurley, Mark Seem, and Helen R. Lane (Minneapolis: University of Minnesota Press, 1983), 33–35, quoted by Theweleit, 1:264–65 (his quotation is emended by my brackets). John Tanke has pointed out that Theweleit incorrectly refers here to "the body with organs." Theweleit's reference to *Anti-Oedipus* clearly indicates that he means "the body without or-

gans'' instead. Deleuze and Guattari define the ''body without organs'' as ''the unproductive, the sterile, the unengendered, the unconsumable'' (8; see also 9–16).

13. David Wallace has pointed out to me that those caught with stolen objects (''with the mainour'') were subject to summary execution.

14. *Chaucer's Sexual Poetics,* 172–73.

15. See the notes to VI.321–22 in Benson, *Riverside Chaucer,* 904.

16. According to a sermon of John Bromyard, the man who is drunk ''farith as it were a queynt candle, and as he were deed in donge.'' Quoted in Owst, *Literature and Pulpit,* 431.

17. ''Inter urinas et faeces nascimur,'' which Freud quotes from St. Augustine. See Sigmund Freud, *Civilization and Its Discontents,* trans. James Strachey (New York: Norton, 1961), 52. I thank James W. Earl for help on this point.

18. One could theorize lack from Lacanian or Augustinian perspectives, but my focus is the Pardoner's success in creating lack and then filling it, a process which turns not so much on lack as on the function of lack in prompting desire. There is a Lacanian reading in Dinshaw, *Chaucer's Sexual Poetics;* see, e.g., 165–67.

19. Dinshaw, *Chaucer's Sexual Poetics,* 176.

20. Derek Pearsall, *The Canterbury Tales* (London: Allen & Unwin, 1985), 94–95.

21. Dinshaw, *Chaucer's Sexual Poetics,* 56–58, 96–99. She cites Claude Lévi-Strauss, *The Elementary Structures of Kinship,* trans. James Harle Bell, et al., rev. ed. (Boston: Beacon, 1969).

22. Luce Irigaray, *This Sex Which Is Not One,* trans. Catherine Porter with Carolyn Burke (Ithaca: Cornell University Press, 1985), 192–93. See Dinshaw, *Chaucer's Sexual Poetics,* 115–20, for references to Irigaray on ''mimicry.''

23. Butler's discussion of Irigaray and the ''masculinist signifying economy'' is one of the most useful I have found; see Judith Butler, *Gender Trouble* (New York; Routledge, 1990), 9–19 (quote from 13).

24. Arthur N. Gilbert, ''Conceptions of Homosexuality and Sodomy in Western History,'' in *Historical Perspectives on Homosexuality,* ed. Salvatore J. Licata and Robert P. Petersen (Binghamton: Haworth, 1985), 65. See also the discussion of sodomy—which was not, of course, limited to homosexual partners—in David F. Greenberg, *The Construction of Homosexuality* (Chicago: University of Chicago Press, 1988), 274–79.

25. Deleuze and Guattari, *Anti-Oedipus,* 35.

26. Jonathan Dollimore, *Sexual Dissidence: Augustine to Wilde, Freud to Foucault* (Oxford: Clarendon, 1991), 182. Jonathan Culler is quoted from *On Deconstruction: Theory and Criticism after Structuralism* (Ithaca: Cornell University Press, 1982), 160.

Contributors

DAVID AERS is Professor of English Literature at the University of East Anglia. His most recent books are *Community, Gender, and Individual Identity in English Writing, 1360–1430* (Routledge, 1988) and *Culture and History, 1350–1600* (Harvester, 1992), which he edited and contributed to. He is working on aspects of Christianity, literature, and politics, 1350–1450.

HELEN T. BENNETT is Associate Professor of English at Eastern Kentucky University, where she teaches Old English and the history of the English language. She has published articles on semiotics, feminism, and Anglo-Saxon studies in journals such as *Exemplaria,* the *Medieval Feminist Newsletter,* and *Semiotica.*

ALLEN J. FRANTZEN, Professor of English at Loyola University of Chicago, is the author of such books as *Desire for Origins: New Language, Old English, and Teaching the Tradition* (Rutgers University Press, 1990) and *The Literature of Penance in Anglo-Saxon England* (Rutgers University Press, 1983). He is now working on a hypertext edition of the Anglo-Saxon penitentials.

BRITTON J. HARWOOD is Professor of English at Miami University, Oxford, and author of Piers Plowman *and the Problem of Belief* (University of Toronto Press, 1992). His chapter is drawn from a book nearing completion on Chaucer and contemporary critical theory, other portions of which have appeared in *Philological Quarterly, PMLA,* the *Review of English Studies,* and *Style.*

HARRIET E. HUDSON is Associate Professor of English at Indiana State University. Her prior publications include "Towards a Theory of Popular Literature: The Case of the Middle English Romances" (*Journal of Popular Culture,* 1989) and "Middle English Popular Romances: The Manuscript Evidence" (*Manuscripta,* 1984).

CLARE A. LEES, Assistant Professor of English at the University of Pennsylvania, has published several articles on Old English homilies, most recently in *Speaking Two Languages: Traditional Disciplines and Contemporary Theory in Medieval Studies* (ed. A. J. Frantzen, SUNY Press, 1991). Review editor since 1988 of the Old English chapter for *The Year's Work in English Studies,* she is editing a collection on medieval masculinities for University of Minnesota Press.

KARMA LOCHRIE is Associate Professor of English at Loyola University of Chicago. The author of *Margery Kempe and Translation of the Flesh* (University of Pennsylvania Press, 1991), she is currently working on a book on secrecy in the middle ages.

GILLIAN R. OVERING is Professor of English at Wake Forest University, where she teaches Old English, linguistics, and women's studies. In addition to articles on Old English literature, literary history, and contemporary theory, she has written *Language, Sign, and Gender in* Beowulf (Southern Illinois University Press, 1990) and is the co-author of *Landscape of Desire: Partial Stories of the Northern Medieval World* (University of Minnesota Press, forthcoming).

JOHN W. TANKE is Assistant Professor of English at the University of Michigan, Ann Arbor. He is currently working on a book entitled "Riddles of Subjectivity in Old English Poetry."

Index